Decorative Techniques
for Transforming
Gourds & Rims

Wax on
GOURDS

Miriam Joy

Schiffer Publishing Ltd®

4880 Lower Valley Road • Atglen, PA 19310

Other Schiffer Books by the Author:

Wax on Crafts: 15 Decorative Techniques for Transforming Your Crafts, ISBN 978-0-7643-5021-4

Wax on Crafts Holiday Projects, ISBN 978-0-7643-4955-3

Miriam Joy's Wax Design Technique, ISBN 978-0-7643-4467-1

Designed by RoS
Cover design by RoS
Type set in Bellota/Candara

ISBN: 978-0-7643-5225-6
Printed in China

Published by Schiffer Publishing, Ltd.
4880 Lower Valley Road
Atglen, PA 19310
Phone: (610) 593-1777; Fax: (610) 593-2002
E-mail: Info@schifferbooks.com
Web: www.schifferbooks.com

For our complete selection of fine books on this and related subjects, please visit our website at www.schifferbooks.com. You may also write for a free catalog.

Schiffer Publishing's titles are available at special discounts for bulk purchases for sales promotions or premiums. Special editions, including personalized covers, corporate imprints, and excerpts, can be created in large quantities for special needs. For more information, contact the publisher.

We are always looking for people to write books on new and related subjects. If you have an idea for a book, please contact us at proposals@schifferbooks.com.

I dedicate this book to the memory of my wonderful sister Robin. Robin was one of a kind. She was strong and never wavered from what she believed or stood for. She was strong in more ways than one. In high school there was not a boy who could beat her at arm wrestling. While she did not always make my life fun when we were little, she sure made up for it when we grew up. She offered me a place of security when I had nowhere else to go. Robin took me in and helped me get started again.

Robin loved kids, all the kids, not just her own. She helped raise several of her nieces and nephews. My kids were no exception. She took care of them, while I went to work. Being a single mom was hard, but it was so much easier knowing they were in good hands.

My daughter was only a couple of years old when Robin moved a few hours away. Cheyenne cried and begged me to let her "commute" to Robin's house for babysitting. Only a city kid would know that word at that young of an age. After that we visited Robin every few months, but we especially loved to go in fall. The kids would get dressed up in their Halloween costumes and we would all go to the pumpkin patch to play and take pictures.

We lost Robin to ovarian cancer but she put on a long, four-year fight. Again she showed all of us what it was like to be strong and brave. The greatest compliment she gave me was telling my son Troy, "No matter how hard life knocks your mom down, she gets up twice as strong." We love you, Robin, and you are greatly missed. I know you are much better off and are sitting in the clouds with the angels, probably making jokes about all of us.

Acknowledgments

I cannot start a book without first acknowledging the Lord Jesus Christ and all the ways He has blessed me. It is because of His love and blessings that any of this is possible. I thank Him for allowing me to shine His light in my little corner of the art world, and for bestowing on me the gift of art that has so richly blessed my life.

To the most wonderful husband in the world, I could not be Miriam Joy without my Buddy Boy. How can I begin to express my love and appreciation for all you do? You are the support crew that keeps me going. I struggle to find the words to express all that you do for me, both as an artist and businesswoman, but most importantly as my partner. You make me feel like the most loved woman in the world. I love our long walks and our heartwarming talks. Sitting with you in the swing with your arms around me and falling asleep at night in your arms. Thank you for being my husband and my best friend. I love you so much.

To the newest addition to the family, our wonderful dog Cody. We did not save you, you saved us. You brought wet kisses and wonderful walks. You patiently sit beside me while I write my book and add a cold nose nudge in every once in a while to make sure I know you are still there. Thanks for adding so much to our lives.

It takes a village to run miriamjoy.com and, trust me, I could not do it without my village. From the people who believed in us and do our manufacturing to our very special friends who help out with products, you are wonderful people. Thank you for all you have done. For all the people who have helped us along the way, friends and family who have prayed for my business, special people who helped edit my books— you guys are the best village a girl could have.

To our children: each one of you has helped in your own special way. You believed in me and have helped me out so much. I cannot thank you enough for your love and support.

Add a little "Joy" to your life!

Contents

Introduction

Our lives are like all the colors in a box of crayons. Sometimes we are blue, or green with envy; other times we are pink with excitement. It would not be life without all the colors.

Have you ever really noticed how many colors are in the tree leaves when they change colors in the fall? It still amazes me every year how awesome God is and how He paints the leaves in red, yellow, orange, brown, green, purple and peach and these are only a few of the many colors in nature, and I am in awe of them all. I hold the colors in my hand and see all the wonder that he has created. That is the way I feel when using all the colors in a crayon box to decorate a gourd. I still get excited and amazed at the beauty of it.

In my book *Miriam Joy's Wax Design,* I covered the basics on how to use the wax design technique on gourds. If you haven't read that book, it is a great one to start with. You'll learn a lot. In this book, I bring you a variety of my best rim treatments as well as fun and colorful gourd designs. The rim treatments are ones that you can use time and time again. Step by step instructions, with lots of pictures, make it easy to learn each. I start by teaching you a simple rim, and then more complex ones.

Along with creating gourds featuring wax designs, you will learn new ways to use the wax, as well as how to make "stones" with the wax. Let's get started!

⸱⸱⸱ Warnings and Precautions ⸱⸱⸱

As with any crafting project, it's important to understand the warnings and precautions as you move through the steps of colorful creation. Note the following:

❶ MJ Low Temp Melting Pot, MJ Wax Design Tools, Embossing Tool, and the MJ Texture Brush Insert can all get very HOT. Use caution and do not touch the hot metal when using or handling these items. Be careful touching items heated with these tools. **They can become very HOT.**

❷ Always have adult supervision in cases where children are using the wax design process. Safety allows fun for everyone! Wax design is not recommended for children under eight years of age.

❸ The MJ Melting pot is an electrical device—caution should be used while using any electrical device.

❹ Use caution when working with a hobby knife: if a tool can cut through a crayon, it can cut you, too!

❺ Unplug the melting pot when not in use. **Do not leave the melting pot unattended!**

Chapter 1
Tools and Supplies

Using Crayola Crayons as Wax

For my wax I use Crayola crayons. Don't you love Crayola crayons? The smell brings back wonderful memories to old and young alike. But seriously, where else can you find all of these colors in one box? And when you start to mix and match all the colors, it becomes unlimited.

Other waxes can be thin and require you to add color, so why not use crayons? It does make a difference for you to use Crayola brand crayons, though. They are brighter, thicker, and the color does not fade. At back-to-school time, you cannot beat the price of a box of twenty-four crayons—my favorite box. It has all the basic colors that I use the most and, as I said, is very cost-effective.

One of the things people are most amazed by is that each color works a little differently. The lighter colors, like yellow and yellow-greens, are thinner in consistency. It is not that you are doing anything wrong as you melt the crayon. The darker colors are a little thicker. Of course, there is one in every bunch that has to make its own rules, and for the Crayola crayons, it is white. The white crayon thinks it is a thicker color and goes on thicker, but can also act like a thinner color and can drip a little more.

When you are working with crayons, the tip of the crayon is the color the wax is going to be. Do not expect your color to come out the color of the label surrounding the crayon. A lot of the darker colors, such as blue or purple, look black when applied as wax. Make the color lighter by adding a sliver of white, until you get the desired color.

Treat your crayons just like paints. Mix and match them in the same way. For example, blue-green and white mixed in equal amounts makes a beautiful turquoise color.

Of course the bigger boxes of crayons have a bigger variety of colors. You start to see gold, silver, bronze, and copper crayons. Just keep in mind that if you are doing a bigger gourd, you may need a couple crayons of the same color. (Colors like inchworm and mac and cheese are among my favorites.) The Crayola Gel FX crayons have bright and vivid colors. There are boxes of metallic and glitter crayons available, too. The metallic crayons have that metallic shine and can add so much to designs or Christmas ornaments. The glitter crayons contain glitter to give projects that extra sparkle. Just remember when using these colors, they add the sparkle and shine, but not the brightness that the regular crayons bring.

Do not be afraid to use old crayons. They do not go bad. Broken, worn, or discarded, they still work great. The end of a school year when kids are throwing away the worn-down or broken crayons and Sunday school programs can be among some of the best places to get unwanted crayons. Also, white is not a favorite color, so it may be easy to come by!

Note: *Read through the varied project instructions I've included for you here in their entirety before beginning.*

Then, if there is a video, though you do not need to view it to work on or complete your project, you may want to; sometimes it's fun to see the design come together before digging in!

Have fun!

The Miriam Joy Product line was created by dreaming. I started playing with wax and realized how amazing it was. I knew that there were so many ways to use it, but I needed tools that I could not find at the craft store. I found that I also wanted to teach other people this wonderful process and to share my love for wax with them. But they, too, needed to be able to get the tools to create beautiful and fun pieces. So I began to create them, one at a time—there were a few fail-and-expensive attempts, but the Miriam Joy tool line began to emerge. The first one was a customized melting pot, followed by the wax tools. Then, to go along with the products, I began to provide YouTube videos for fun projects to help and inspire crafters everywhere. (See www.youtube.com/user/Miriamjoy123).

As I continue to find new ways to use the wax, I continue to make new tools. I hope to keep growing the tool line. To order Miriam Joy Products please visit me at www. MiriamJoy.com.

Note: I try to keep all the customized MJ Products made in the United States where we can also help other artists and companies grow. We have had a lot of people help us along the way, so it is important for Miriam Joy to help others.

MJ Low Temp Melting Pot

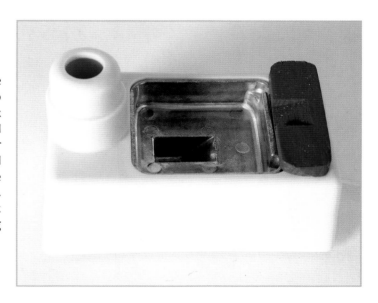

Use an MJ Low Temp Melting Pot to melt the crayons. The melting pot is UL rated and is 120°F, the perfect temperature to melt crayons without getting the wax too hot. Keeping the wax confined to the little well is what allows you to use such a small amount of crayon. The well provides an area for you to dip your wax tool. Most melting pots are round or other shapes. It would take around twenty crayons to fill up other melting pots because they do not have a well, which is what makes this process work. I have tried several other items and methods to melt my wax and have had no success when using the tools. The MJ Melting Pot is customized to keep your tool in the well.

MJ Texture Brush and Insert

MJ Texture Brush and Insert

The MJ Texture Brush and Insert is designed to create textured backgrounds: trees, bushes, and grass. It also makes wonderful snow.

Insert placed into the melting pot

Directions: The insert is placed on top of the MJ Melting Pot when the melting pot is empty. After the insert has warmed, melt the crayon on the insert. Use your MJ Texture Brush to apply the melting crayon onto your project.

While the MJ Texture Brush was designed for wax, it works great with paints as well.

I have made a video to help you with this process at:
http://youtu.be/1oORrPRGOBo

9

MJ Wax Design Tools

I have designed a line of MJ Wax Tools and have had them manufactured just for this process. They each have a foam handle to keep them from getting warm while being held. The foam handle also makes them comfortable to hold. The tools are well-balanced. There are four MJ Wax Design Tools. Each tool has two different sized tips, so that it is like getting two tools in each one, and who doesn't love a two for one deal?

The type of metal for these tools does matter. Aluminum tools will not work with this process, as aluminum does not hold the heat evenly and the wax does not stick to the tool. Wooden-handle tools do not hold the heat as well, and the wood handle gets very warm. After heating and cooling the wood handle tools, the tips tend to come unglued from the wood. On the MJ tool, the balls on each end hold the wax on the tool. A lot of thought and trial and error went into designing these tools. I have found that people who have had a hard time holding other tools, due to arthritis and other medical conditions, find these tools easier to use.

MJ Wax Design Tool #2 is the tool I designed first, and is still the tool I use the most and the first tool that I start my students with. If you can only start with one tool, this is the one I recommend.

- MJ Wax Design Tool #2 is ³⁄₁₆" on one end and ¼" on the other end. Tools bigger than this size drip a little too much.
- MJ Wax Design Tool #1 is a step down from the #2 tool. If you want a medium-sized stroke, this is a tool for you. MJ Wax Design Tool #1 is ⅛" on one end and ⁵⁄₃₂" on the other end.
- MJ Wax Design Tool #0 is a smaller tool and used for smaller work. It creates smaller strokes. MJ Wax Design Tool #0 is ²⁄₂₅" on one end and ¹⁄₁₀" on the other end.
- MJ Wax Design Tool #00 is the smallest of the tools. This tool is designed for fine detail work or where other strokes cannot fit. The size of the tool is ³⁄₆₄" on one end and .072" on the other end.

The size of the tool you use determines the size of the stroke or dot. If you need a larger, longer stroke or dot, use a bigger tool. If you need a little or short stroke or dot, use a smaller tool. If you need fine tiny details, use the MJ Wax Design Tool #00.

MJ Wax Design Tool sitting in melting pot

MJ Wax Brushes

MJ Wax Brushes were designed to apply a layer of melted wax.

Directions: The brush is dipped into the well of the melting pot to pick up wax. This is one of the times that you can fill the melting pot above the well if you like. While the wax is still warm, apply it to your project. You can apply a second coat if needed. Let the first coat harden or cool and then reapply.

You do use more wax with this method. I do not clean these brushes. They are inexpensive enough to keep one for each color. I have also added foam to this brush to make it easier to handle and to keep it from getting warm. To straighten the bristles when using a brush with cold wax in the bristles, set the brush into the well of the melting pot to re-warm the wax.

Load your MJ Wax Brush with wax from the melting pot well.

There is a video to help you with this process at:
http://youtu.be/mp7rpBmRAS0

MJ Wax Liner

The wax liner is used for those times when you really need to make a straight line. You can write with it, make very small dots, or use it to outline your artwork to make it look fresh. It makes great pine needles for trees.

Directions: Place the wax liner into the melting pot well with melted wax; allow it to warm for forty-five seconds to a minute. Once warm, scoop up the wax and tool and you are ready to begin your project. As long as you warmed your tool long enough, you will be able to write for quite a while before it stops. When the wax runs out, or the wax cools, set the wax liner back into the well to re-warm. To clean the tool, dump all of the wax out. Wipe the outside with a paper towel. Take a Q-tip and push it into the well of the wax liner to remove any remaining wax.

Load wax into an MJ Wax Liner.

There is a video to help you with this process at:
http://youtu.be/5GcYQNMhdAo

MJ Three Pot Tray

I've designed a tray that holds the melting pots in place. This makes the melting pots more secure and less likely to move. I suggest you place the electrical cords going away from you so that you do not get tangled up in them. Then hook them up to a single power cord with multiple outlets and an on/off switch on the cord so you can turn them on and off with ease at the same time. The red light on the power strip also lets you know if the melting pots are still on.

The tray has a lip to help keep everything contained. The tray helps keep the wax off you. If the wax is going to drip, it will most likely drip here. By the way, I recommend working in an old shirt or an apron since crayon is hard to get out of your clothes.

There is a video to help you with this process at:
http://youtu.be/6oIoXDV-Iq8

MJ Dry Board

The MJ Dry Board has little plastic spikes so that you can continue to dry your gourd after you have colored or varnished it without the gourd sticking to the board.

Directions: You should not spray varnish on the MJ Dry Board. Varnish the project first and then place it onto the board to continue drying.

There is a video to help you with this process at:
http://youtu.be/Mu9uv_dtJoA

Rubber Rulers

The MJ Flex-e rulers come in two sizes. The one-yard length is available in both a 1" width and a ½" width, great for measuring around the rim of a gourd. There is also a shorter 12" by ½" ruler called the MJ Mini Flex-e.

The rubber helps hold the ruler in place so you can measure items with ease. Just place the Flex-e around the gourd and put a little tension on the ruler, and it will hold in place while you measure.

There is a video to show you how to use the Flex-e at:
http://youtu.be/xEhY2j-zm7M

MJ Craft Templates

MJ Craft Templates were invented first, out of my frustration at not being able to create the perfect shape; and second, out of my desire to find a better way to create designs or trace more exacting patterns. While other templates are made of plastic or paper and are contained all on one sheet, the MJ Craft Templates are made of flexible rubber and can be used on round or square objects. They are the first templates that can go around the corner of a wall. These templates are great for many crafting needs, such as school projects, quilting, woodworking, stained-glass work and gourding—just to name a few. The MJ Craft Templates are made of ¹⁄₁₆"-rubber and come in a variety of shapes and sizes. The rubber allows the templates to hold in place without slipping while tracing the shape.

There is a video to show you how to use the craft templates at:
http://youtu.be/nc09fhVwBbY

Basic Supplies

Removable Glue Dots

Removable glue dots are used when you need a little help holding the craft template in place or if the templates are larger than you can easily hold with one hand while marking. I cut the glue dots in half to fit the craft template, thus making the package of glue dots go twice as far.

Directions: Apply glue dots to at least four places on the template. Place the template on your project and trace your shape. Remove the template and pull off the glue dots. It is important to use removable glue dots: they are designed with removal in mind.

Mr. Clean Magic Eraser®

I have found that a Mr. Clean Magic Eraser makes removing the charcoal pencil lines easy. They can be found in the bathroom cleaning supply section at most stores. I cut my sponge into three sections; it is a bit easier to use this way and lasts a little longer.

Directions: Wet it slightly and wring out all the water. Wipe the area that shows the charcoal pencil. This will leave a chalky white film behind. Lightly dampen a paper towel and remove the film.

There is a video to help you with this process at:
http://youtu.be/voGnUzpENYI

Embossing Tool

The embossing tool is also called a heat gun, and can be found in the scrapbook section of the craft stores. Use the embossing tool to reheat the wax in a method I call twice melted, or for heat setting some inks used in gourd art.

Hobby Knife with Shovel Blade

I use a hobby knife with a shovel nose blade to remove unwanted wax. It allows you to maneuver in between your strokes when removing crayon, so that if you make a mistake or if you have an unwanted drop of wax, you can simply remove it.

Directions: Always use your hobby knife at an angle when removing wax. Holding the knife with the blade straight up and down causes scratching to occur. Start at the biggest end of the stroke or drop and work toward the small end. This allows you to get under the wax more easily and you can remove more of the wax this way.

If you need to remove any stain left behind from the wax, use a gum eraser. (If you are going to put another stroke on at that spot, and the stain won't show, just don't worry about the stain.)

There is a video to help you with this process at:
http://youtu.be/fGNg21bfb2A

White Charcoal Pencil

To trace the shapes onto your gourd, I use a white charcoal pencil. It leaves a bright enough line to see easily and can be removed. Unlike some craft pencils, you can put the charcoal pencil in a pencil sharpener to sharpen it.

Directions: If the pencil is not leaving a dark enough line, simply take the pencil and use a flame from a cigarette lighter, or other type of flame, to warm the pencil tip. This makes that pencil line bright and removes any wax buildup that you may have on the pencil.

Cleanup Supplies

Of course, the most important items are the cleanup supplies. These make cleaning a breeze. Cotton balls are used to absorb the crayon and clean the MJ Melting Pot. Cotton swabs are used to clean the MJ Wax Liner. Damp Q-tips can also be used to remove charcoal pencil lines in hard-to-get-to areas. Paper towels are used to wipe and clean your MJ Wax Design Tools as well as to clean the MJ Texture Brush and Insert.

Acrylic Paints

Most of the gourd projects in this book were base-coated with acrylic paints. I love using lots of methods to color my gourds, but I generally find myself using acrylic paints for my more advanced gourd designs.

Directions: To base-coat a gourd, use at least two coats until there is one solid color of paint. Make sure the paint is very dry before applying a second coat. The nice thing about using acrylic paints with wax design is that you can later touch up any mistakes you have made, and it will blend right in.

Varnish, Glaze, Lacquer, and Epoxy Resin

For the wax process, I use different finishes for different gourds, depending on how much the gourd is going to be handled, or if the gourd is flat; or whether it will be exposed to the sun.

Spray-on varnish works great, but a lot of people are intimidated by sprays. Do not let spray varnishes worry you—just try it. Practice until you get comfortable. Runs can be caused by getting too close or going too slowly when varnishing. Varnish in a ventilated area. If you are working outside in the sun, remember that you are working with wax and you cannot leave it in the sun to dry.

Directions: Start by shaking your can to mix the varnish. Spray about twelve inches away from your gourd. Start on one side of your gourd, working in a back-and-forth motion. Do not use a circular motion. It does not cover evenly. Place your gourd on the MJ Dry Board so that it can continue to dry without sticking to the gourd. Once the varnish dries to the touch, apply another coat. Applying varnish not only protects the wax, but also brings

out the color of the wax (crayon). Apply several coats.

The humidity can cause your varnish to turn white. That is why I like to use gloss. It is less likely to turn white. If your varnish should turn white, let it dry and varnish it again on a dryer day to turn it back to its original state.

You can use brush-on varnish if you have used acrylic paint or have heat set your dyes so they will not run. Brush-on varnish can pick up the dye or color and bring it over your wax, so make sure that, when using it, your color has been heat set before you apply your wax design. Brush-on varnishes are usually thicker and result in better coverage.

I like to use several layers of Polycrylic. Another product, Triple Thick by Americana, is also available as a brush-on varnish. Triple Thick is very thick varnish and covers very well. Another option to help keep the wax from melting is marine varnish. It is very thick and hard when dry. I would still do at least two to three coats. The drawback to marine varnish is that it has a yellow tint to it. Also, it's not water-based, so you have to clean your brush with turpentine.

I use glazes and lacquer on some of my small gourd projects. It seems to go on well and does not show too much. I also use it over jewelry pieces to keep them from melting in the sun. When applying a thick glaze or lacquer product, it helps if the surface it's being applied to is flat so the product stays level while it dries. All of the wax must be covered. This sometimes can take more than one coat. Apply it by starting on the outside and working your way toward the middle. You can also apply it by putting it into a bowl and brushing it on.

Remember to always test your products first on a small, inconspicuous place on the gourd. I test mine on the bottom of the gourd where it won't show. Manufacturers are always changing formulas, and even if it's a type of finish you've used in the past, testing on a small area assures that you will be happy with your finished surface.

Chapter 2
Preparing Your Gourd

Cleaning the Gourd

Gourds grow with a waxy "skin" that must be removed. The skin often is moldy and dirty. If the skin is not completely removed, some of your wax will not stick, and neither will varnish or sealer. The completed design may look good initially, but in a few months it will start peeling and chipping.

You can buy gourds that are already cleaned, as well as cut, from some gourd farmers. This is nice if you want to get them ready to go.

If you buy a gourd that has not been cleaned, soak it in warm water and clean it with a copper wire scourer. Allow it to dry thoroughly.

Some people have mold allergies, so take precautions such as wearing a mask and making sure of adequate ventilation when cleaning, sawing, sanding, and handling unclean gourds.

There is a video to help you with this process at:
http://youtu.be/EqOIZs_45Rs

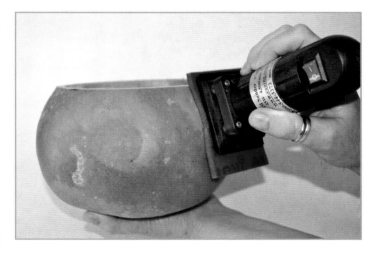

Sanding (or Not)

Many gourd artists sand their gourds before adding color and art. Sanding helps ensure the surface is truly clean; however, it can be made *too* smooth for the wax design process. I do sand away any scratches, dirt, or scars, but I don't overdo it. To adhere, the wax needs some "tooth" on the surface.

Cutting the Gourd

One way to cut a gourd is to use a jigsaw. First you need to mark your line. You can use the MJ Craft Templates or Flex-e to help. Trace the line on with the white charcoal pencil.

To start the cut, you can drill a hole or make one with your hobby knife. Then insert the blade of your jigsaw. (There are also lots of saws out there made specifically to cut gourds.) To keep the jigsaw from kicking back, keep pressure on the saw against the gourd. Saw along the line, continuing until you reach the point where you started. If you like you can sand the cut rim to make it smooth.

There is a video to help you with this process at:
http://youtu.be/MOtPvlMsWhE

Cleaning the Inside

Remove any large parts that are loose. Use a scraper to clean the inside of the gourd. Start at the bottom of the gourd and pull up to the top. Continue around until you have completed the whole gourd.

There is a video to help you with this process at:
http://youtu.be/S5Z5-gtB_qY

Spray Painting the Inside

I use the most inexpensive black matte spray paint I can find to spray the inside of the gourd. Shake the spray paint well to mix it. Wear latex gloves when spraying to keep the paint off your hands.

Hold the spray paint can inside the gourd. Do not pull it out past the rim. Spray the bottom and the sides; this is the one time that you can spray closer than twelve inches. The inside surface of the gourd is very absorbent and the paint goes on well.

Do not try to spray the rim. That is when overspray gets on the gourd. If you do get overspray on your rim, take your damp Mr. Clean Magic Eraser and rub until the paint is removed.

If the gourd is too tall and you can't reach the bottom of it with the spray paint, take black acrylic paint, add a little water to thin it, then pour it in the gourd and swish it around. Make sure that you don't use too much thinned paint because you do not want to have to pour the excess out—doing so often makes a mess. Use only enough to cover the bottom surface and absorb into the gourd.

Now use a brush to paint the rim with black acrylic paint. Painting it gives it a nice even color.

I don't like to use spray paint on the outside of my gourd. The paint can sometimes bubble and that creates a different texture to do wax work on.

There is a video to help you with this process at:
https://youtu.be/1luE0uo8eoc

Chapter 3
Learning the Basics of Wax Design

Setting Up Your Tray

1.

Place your MJ Low Temp Melting Pots into the tray.

Place the cords away from you to keep yourself from getting tangled in them. I use a power strip to keep the melting pots plugged into, so that I do not have to unplug all of the melting pots individually. I can just flip the switch and turn them off and on. If you have a red light on the power strip, it helps to keep track whether they are off or on.

Fold your paper towel into fours. Place it in the right-hand bottom corner and place your tools on top.

To the left of the bottom tray, keep the craft knife and white charcoal pencil so they will always be handy.

2.

Next, plug in your MJ Low Temp Melting Pot and get it warmed up. This only takes a few minutes, and you can load your crayon while it is still warming. Remember to use only Crayola brand crayons. (I will refer to Crayola crayons as wax, which is what they are.)

Holding the crayon with the tip pointed up, cut the crayon paper just above the word "Crayola."

3.

With your hobby knife, cut the paper down the side of the crayon to where you first cut the paper. Do not try to peel the paper back with the knife. It is much harder that way and you are more likely to cut yourself.

4.

Peel the paper off the crayon to where you cut it with the hobby knife. I leave the rest of the paper on my crayon. This keeps it clean and keeps from getting other colors on the crayon. I also leave the name of the crayon as the last part so that if I need to know what color it is, I have that information.

5.

Take your scissors and cut the crayon just above where you cut the paper.

6.

Cut that piece in half with your scissors. By breaking the crayon into two pieces, they fit into the well of the melting pot. It keeps the crayon from melting on the top layer of the well and wasting your wax.

7.

Put both pieces into the well. It is okay to get some of the crayon on the next level of the well—it just helps to keep it cleaner and avoids waste.

There is a video you can watch to show you how to cut and add the crayon at:
http://youtu.be/64wt_GAWB3s

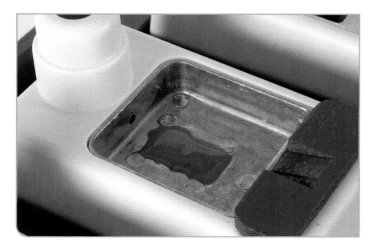

Your melted crayon should not overflow into the second level.

8.

Your melted crayon should not overflow into the second level. You want to make sure that you do not fill the well too full unless you are working with the glass eyedropper or the MJ Wax Brushes. If the well is so full that you cannot see the rectangle of the well, you will start to drip more when working with the MJ Wax Tools. If you fill the well too full, simply take a cotton ball and absorb a little crayon.

There is a video to help you know if you have too much crayon in the well at: **http://youtu.be/S6bcOZJoIZg**

9.

It is important to keep the well full. Do not let your well get less than three-quarters full. This helps keep your strokes the same size because you are picking up the same amount of wax. If you notice your strokes getting smaller, check the level of your wax.

10.

To add crayon to your well, take your scissors and cut the size of crayon piece you may need. I leave the paper on when I am doing this. A lot of times once it is cut, it comes out of the paper all by itself; if not, then cut the paper with your hobby knife and remove it.

There is a video to help you know when to add more crayon to your well at: **http://youtu.be/LBQatFU1dnY**

Absorb just a little crayon with the cotton ball if the well is too full.

The right amount of wax in the well.

The level of wax when you need to add more crayon.

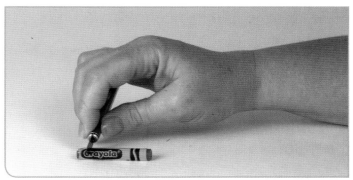

Keep the well full by adding more crayon as needed.

Loading Your Tool

1.

Preheat your tool. **THIS IS THE MOST IMPORTANT INFORMATION TO MAKE THIS PROCESS WORK!** If you do not warm your tools and try to apply warm wax with a cold tool, you will get a glob of wax. The wax will stick to the tool and not want to come off. It only takes about fifteen seconds or more to warm the tool. If the area you are working in is cooler, the tool may need a few seconds longer to warm.

2.

Make sure that the project you are working on is not cold. This will cause the wax not to work correctly. If your item is cold, allow it to warm up to room temperature. You can also warm it up with a blow dryer or embossing tool.

    Start with the small end of the MJ Wax Design Tool #2. This is the easier of the tools to begin with.

Warm your tools by placing them in the wax.

3.

Place the tool into your wax and warm the end of your tool.

4.

Once your MJ Wax Design Tool is warm, place it in the deepest part of the well. Go all the way to the bottom. Touch the bottom and pull your tool straight out. By pulling it straight up, you get the maximum amount of wax. Do not pull the tool out slowly or come up along the side of the well. This removes some of the wax.

    Watch yourself the first few times you load your strokes, as it is an instinct to want to knock off the drip of wax. You will not even realize that you are doing this. You want the drip—the drip is what adds texture to your stroke. Be careful not to form the bad habit of stirring the wax excessively, clicking or hitting the sides of the well. The crayon should only be stirred if it has been sitting a while and the color has separated. White crayons need stirring a little more often, as do metallic and glitter crayons. The easiest way to do this is to not overthink it. Just go to the deepest part of the well, touch the bottom, and pull the tool straight out. Make sure that you load it in the same spot each time, as this will keep your strokes consistent in size.

Place your tool in the deepest part of the well and pull straight up.

5.

Know where you are going with your stroke before you pick it up. Do not load the wax and sit there and hold it while you are looking where to go. This cools your wax and your stroke will not go on smoothly. It is natural to get excited after putting on a stroke—while still holding the tool in your hand and allowing the tool to cool. Watch out for this. (I am the worst offender of holding the tool in my hand while talking to someone.) If you get distracted, just let the tool warm up again before your next stroke.

6.

Keep the project you are working on no farther than twelve inches from the melting pot. Any farther and your tool will start to cool off. If you notice a drip, see how far your project is from the melting pot. If drips continue, check to see if you are sitting in front of a breeze, like that from a fan, heater, or air conditioner.

There is a video to help you with this process at:
http://youtu.be/7TWjiINf3kQ

How to Make a Stroke

1.

Pick up a pencil and hold it in your hand as if you are going to write on something. See how you are holding the pencil sideways, while resting your hand on the paper. This is how you should hold the tool. By

resting the side of your hand on your project surface, you gain control of the stroke. Do not try to hold your tool straight up and down or try to balance it with your little finger. Resting the heel of your hand will give you balance, you will have control over your stroke, and your lines will come out consistently straight. If you try to make the strokes with the tool straight up and down, without resting your hand on the surface, your strokes will wobble all over the place. Now pull the pencil toward you in a straight line.

2.

Start by practicing your strokes on a piece of gourd. Load your tool with the wax: going to the deepest part of the well, touch the bottom and bring it straight out. Bring it to your gourd piece. Make sure not to go too fast, because that will cause the wax to drip. With your hand sideways the way you would hold a pencil, and keeping your hand resting on the gourd piece, pull the stroke toward you. Slowly set the tool on the gourd piece, pulling it toward you until it runs out of wax. Most people lift the tool too early. Make sure you pull, pull, pull that stroke. You are starting with a lot of wax and going until you run out of wax. Pulling the stroke until it runs out of wax results in a great tail on the stroke. Remember to always pull the stroke until it runs out or is stopped short by a pattern design.

There is a video to help you with this process at:
http://youtu.be/imRRnLwBdkw

3.

Make sure that you are pulling your stroke nice and easy. Do not skim the top of the gourd with the tool. Set the tool down and pull your stroke nice and slow. Pulling it too fast makes the wax skip. The slower you pull the stroke, the longer the stroke will become. If you notice that the edges of your strokes are uneven and are not smooth, you need to warm your tool a little more. Make sure when you are pulling your stroke that you do not twist the tool. This picks up wax from the back and makes the tail of the stroke uneven. Never go back over a stroke you do not like. The wax is already cooling and it will just make a mess.

There is a video to help you with this process at:
http://youtu.be/PH8tSEQYBJo

4.

Remember that the length and the width of the stroke are controlled by the size of the tool you use: the bigger the tool, the bigger the stroke; the smaller the tool, the smaller the stroke. You must reload for each stroke no matter how big or small the stroke is.

How to Make a Dot

Dots are loaded the same as a stroke. The size of the tool determines the size of the dot. Load the tool each time you make a dot. Do not think that you can load your tool anywhere in the well. Make sure that you go to the bottom of the well when loading the wax. This helps keep the dots consistent in size. You can also do a descending dot, which is a lot of fun. Load your tool and dot, dot, dot. Each successive dot will be smaller because you are running out of wax. I use this method a lot in my designs. You can do designs with just dots. You will also notice little tiny flecks of wax when you do the dots. The bigger the dot, the more flecks you get. If you are getting more than two flecks per dot, then slow down. You can remove them with your hobby knife or leave them depending on the texture of your design. Apply dots to areas that need cleaning up, like the ends of strokes or to help fill in an open area.

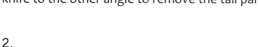

There is a video to help you with this process at:
http://youtu.be/7fGqF5YDpMI

How to Remove a Stroke, Dot, or Drop

Use a shovel tip on the hobby knife to remove a stroke, dot, or drop. The shovel tip lets you get in between your strokes and remove the wax you do not want. Allow the wax to harden or cool. Trying to remove wax while it is liquid is harder and can smear the color of the crayon, making a bigger mess to clean up.

1.

Put the hobby knife under the largest part of the stroke or dot. Starting with the largest part of the stroke will get a bigger piece of the wax off.

Always hold the hobby knife at an angle. Do not hold the knife straight up and down or scratches will occur. Turn the knife to the other angle to remove the tail part of the stroke.

2.

When you are removing the wax, you should not be able to hear any sound. If you hear scraping sounds, try a lighter touch.

If you need to remove any stain left behind from the wax, do so with a gum eraser. If you are going to put a stroke back on, do not worry about the stain, unless it would show.

There is a video to help you with this process at:
http://youtu.be/fGNg21bfb2A

How to Make Freehand Strokes

Now that you've learned how to do a basic stroke and dots, you are going to learn how to curve the strokes.

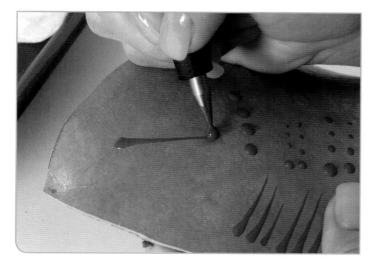

1.

Start out with a straight stroke down the middle. Remember to pull that stroke nice and long and do not lift up the wax tool until it runs out of wax.

2.

The first stroke you put on is already starting to cool. Cold wax does not like to cross over cold wax. But you can cross over the bottom half of the stroke, since there is not much wax there. So pull a curved stroke from the right side, meeting up with the first stroke and pulling the tail next to the tail of the first stroke. Pull until you run out of wax.

3.

Repeat what you just did, this time starting on the left side and meeting up at the middle.

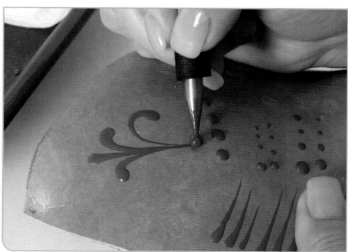

4.

Try a little freehand work. Go back to the right side, farther out, and pull a stroke. Really curve it this time. Meet up with the tails of the other strokes a little farther down.

5.

Switch to a smaller tool. Pull a curved stroke inside the stroke you just did. Meet up with the tails in the middle.

See how easy it is to add strokes? Where do you think you need another stroke? Should it be straight, curved, or really curved? Complete the design by adding dots or descending dots where you think you need just a little something. Use dots to fill in open areas.

Starting to get the hang of it? Try something different. What types of designs do you see?

> There is a video to help you with this process at:
> **https://youtu.be/sP9xooAWlOk**

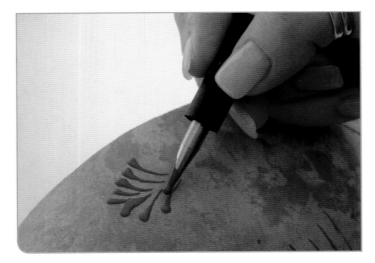

Practice Makes Perfect

You should practice until you are comfortable with your strokes, dots, and drops. Also practice removing them. Try different tools to make different sized strokes and dots. Some people find that a certain size tool works better for them and is easier to use. Make sure that you try both ends of each MJ Wax Design tool.

Know that each Crayola color will work differently. The darker colors contain more pigments and will make bigger strokes because they are thicker. With the thinner colors, like yellow, you can pull the stroke farther. Learn the colors and how they work. Take the colors that you want to use and pull them with each

tool so that you know how long that color will pull and what size stroke it will make.

Practice until your strokes become consistent in size. Remember to load the tool in the well in the same way every time. If your strokes start to get smaller, check the crayon level in the well.

Remember that you are your own worst critic. If you do not like a stroke, then remove it. If it bugs you, take it off!

> There is a good video that helps you
> with all the basics and is a good refresher course at:
> **http://youtu.be/cR5Tmi-kJ5E**

Chapter 4
Cleaning Your Tools

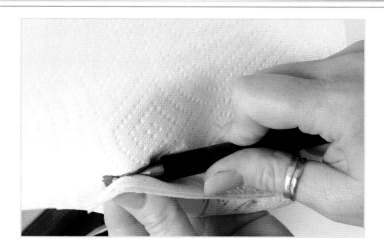

How to Clean the MJ Wax Design Tools

Cleaning your MJ Wax Design Tools is easy. Simply take a paper towel and wipe off the tool while it is still warm. You will need to do this before you use a new color. It you let the wax harden on the tool, removing the wax becomes difficult. Place your tool back into the wax to warm it again and wipe it on the paper towel. I keep my paper towel folded into fours, making it easier to use.

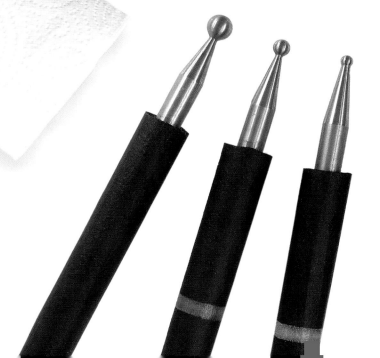

How to Clean the MJ Melting Pot

1.

To change colors or clean your melting pot, simply take a cotton ball and pull it in half. Keep it in balls.

2.

Take the first half of the cotton ball and place it into the well. I use the MJ Wax Design Tool #0, because it can get into tight corners. Do not touch the metal with your fingers. The metal is hot. Using the wax tool, slowly push the cotton ball into the well. If you push the cotton ball too fast, the color comes out the sides, making a bigger mess. Going slower allows the wax to absorb as it goes. Lift the cotton ball out with your wax tool. Start at the front of the well, get under the cotton ball, and pull it out.

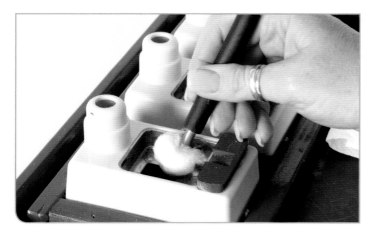

3.

Take the other half of the cotton ball and, using the wax tool, clean off the top part of the well. Finish by cleaning the inside of the well. You will be amazed how easy it is to clean. The cleaning is done while the melting pot is still plugged in.

    Once you have cleaned the well, you can put your new color into the well to melt.

4.

The crayon can be left in the well and used again later. Just plug the melting pot back in when you are ready to use it and wait for it to melt before you start. If you are done with the color, unplug the melting pot and let the color cool. When the wax is hard, plug the melting pot back in. It will start to melt on the sides. This happens very fast. Take your hobby knife and push it between the top of the well and the color will pop out in a block.

There is a video to help you with this process at:
http://youtu.be/FKQKi-Y9lhs

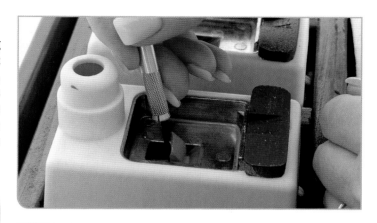

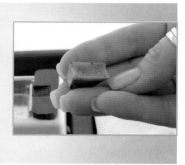

You can reuse the color block. It never goes bad. Just pop it in a bag and use it next time. To reuse it, start by adding the block of color to your melting pot first then add any additional wax needed to fill the well.

How to Clean the MJ Texture Brush

1.

To clean your MJ Texture Brush and Insert, start by melting the crayon in your brush on the insert.

2.

Use a paper towel to wipe the insert while it is in the melting pot.

There is a video to help you with this process at:
http://youtu.be/qwwYk4_agoE

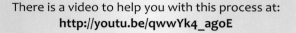

3.

Set the MJ Texture Brush on the insert to melt the crayon. Wipe the MJ Texture Brush on the paper towel. Keep repeating until the crayon is melted out.

4.

To clean the brush completely, spray with a degreaser like Awesome®. Clean the brush again on the insert in the melting pot until all the color is gone. Rinse with warm water.

Chapter 5
Flowers in the Jungle

✓Supply List

- ☐ —Bottle gourd, cut and cleaned (exterior cleaned and lightly sanded, cut edge smooth, interior painted)
- ☐ —#2 MJ Wax Design Tool
- ☐ —#1 MJ Wax Design Tool
- ☐ —one or more wax melting pots
- ☐ —MJ Circle Craft Templates
- ☐ —Flex-e Ruler
- ☐ —MJ Dry Board
- ☐ —tray
- ☐ —drill and ¼" drill bit
- ☐ —jigsaw or gourd saw
- ☐ —gourd compass
- ☐ —Staybowlizer
- ☐ —Crayola crayons in colors Inchworm, Cotton Candy, Razzle Dazzle Rose, Sky Blue Gel FX, Dandelion, and Orange
- ☐ —black acrylic paint
- ☐ —black spray paint
- ☐ —varnish
- ☐ —strand of shells, beads or stones
- ☐ —embroidery needle
- ☐ —black artificial sinew or waxed linen
- ☐ —superglue
- ☐ —paintbrush
- ☐ —scissors
- ☐ —hobby knife
- ☐ —white charcoal pencil
- ☐ —Mr. Clean Magic Easier
- ☐ —cotton balls
- ☐ —Q-tips
- ☐ —paper towels
- ☐ —water container

Preparing the Gourd

For this project I used a bottle gourd. You could use any type of gourd you like. The pattern can be applied easily to any shape. You might prefer it on a different type of gourd or, if you grow your own gourds, you may have a type of gourd that you have a lot of.

Mark the top of the gourd with a gourd compass. Leave at least 2" to 3" on the top part of the gourd if using a bottle gourd so that you have room to put flowers in that space. Cut the top with your jigsaw or gourd saw.

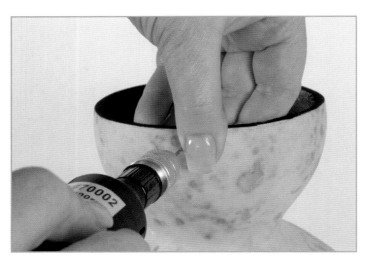

Mark a line ¼" down from the cut edge. You can use a divider, compass, or a Flex-e ruler to help you measure. Mark the holes ¾" apart around the rim. The drill bit needs to be big enough that you can stick your threaded needle through the hole with no problem. For this project I used a ¼" drill bit.

Another way to measure, for times when it does not have to be precise, is to place your thumb and drill to the right of your thumb. Move your thumb to the other side of the hole and drill again. This is a fast and easy way and turns out pretty even most of the time.

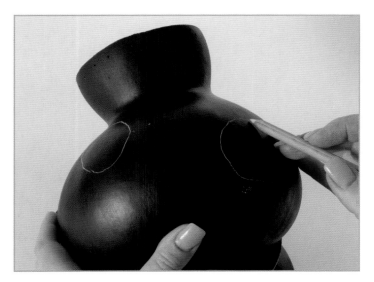

Paint the exterior of the gourd with two coats of black acrylic paint. Any brand is fine. (I do not spray paint the outside of the gourd. I do not like the texture spray paint leaves, and it can bubble or peel.)

Take the white charcoal pencil and draw circles here and there on the gourd. Make the circles about 3" in diameter (optional: use an MJ circle Craft Template). The flowers don't need to be perfectly round; some can be a little oblong. Make sure to put some circles on the top of the gourd too. Do not apply too many flowers; you want to leave enough room for the big fern leaves. Don't place any circles on the bottom of the gourd.

"Flowers in the Jungle" Wax Design

The Crayola Crayon colors that I used for this project are Inchworm, Cotton Candy, Razzle Dazzle Rose, and Sky Blue Gel FX crayon. These colors were from a box of 96 crayons. I usually stick to the box of 24 crayons because they are the cheapest and easiest to find, but for this project I wanted bright fluorescent colors. You can use any colors that you like and that go well with the background color you choose. I chose black for the background so the flowers would stand out.

1.

Draw a flat oval with the white charcoal pencil in the middle of the flower. This is the center. It helps shape the flower. You will be using Sky Blue Gel FX crayon for the first flower. The gel crayons have bright and wonderful colors but can drip a little more than other types. I used an MJ Wax Design Tool #2 small end because I wanted bigger flower petals. If the crayon is dripping too much or you have a smaller flower, use a smaller tool. Pull the first petal down from the top half of the flower to the middle. Stop when you meet the oval line middle.

Start to the right of the first stroke. Leave enough room that the strokes do not run together. Pull this stroke with a slight curve to the left and stop when you reach the middle. Adding the curve to the stroke makes it look more like a flower.

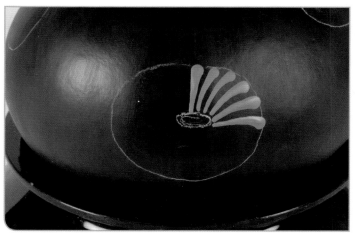

2.

Continue to add more petals following the outside of the circle. Add more curve as you go. Stop each stroke when you reach the middle. Do about a quarter of the flower. Repeat on the other side of the flower, curving the strokes to the right.

3.

Starting where you left off on both sides, continue adding strokes toward the middle. Add more curve the closer you get to the middle bottom of the flower.

In case you are wondering what the gourd in this photo is sitting on, it's a Staybowlizer, a kitchen item that can be ordered online. It is great for holding gourds steady while you're working on them.

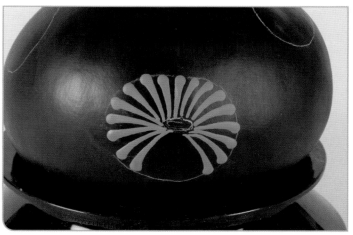

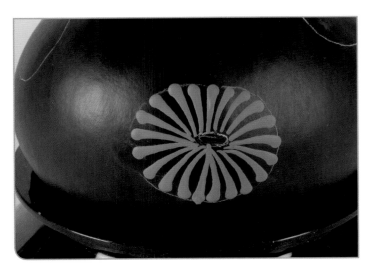

4.

The last stroke in the middle of the bottom of the flower is going to be straight. Turn your gourd upside down and pull the stroke toward you. You may find it easier to put the last couple of strokes in after you put the middle stroke in.

Check to see how many flowers you have. Plan it out so that you'll have a couple of flowers of each color. Try not to have two of the same color beside each other. Remember the ones on the top of the gourd when figuring this out. Create all of the "blue" flowers in the same way.

7.

Flip your gourd over and find the MJ Circle Craft Template that fits the bottom of the gourd where it sits. You do not want to put wax on the bottom of the gourd. You can use the Staybowlizer as a reference. Mark the bottom of the gourd with the white charcoal pencil, just above the Staybowlizer. Another way to find the bottom of the gourd is to set the gourd upright and trace around the bottom of the gourd where it touches the surface of the table. Match that line up with a Circle Craft Template. Trace inside the template with a white charcoal pencil.

5.

The next color you are going to use is Razzle Dazzle Rose. If you are working with one melting pot, clean it out and put in the new color. Do all of the rose-colored flowers in the same way.

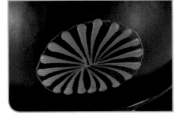

6.

The color for the last flower is Cotton Candy. This color is not as opaque as the other colors; you might prefer a more opaque color such as Carnation Pink or a purple like Wisteria. Use the colors you like, or if you're making this gourd to give as a gift, colors that the recipient may like.

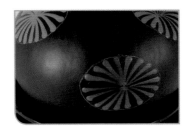

8.

Starting at the bottom of the gourd, draw a line with the white charcoal pencil between the flowers, coming up to the neck of the gourd. This is the center vein for the fern leaves. Start at the next section between the flowers and have some lines go under and some on top of the flowers. The lines should not be straight up and down. They should be curving around the flowers. Have a line branch off to fill in a section between two flowers. Some lines might be shorter and only curve around part of a flower from the bottom of the gourd. Each line should be different. Fill in all the open areas with at least one line.

9.

Clean out your melting pot and add Inchworm. If you do not have Inchworm, yellow-green is a good substitute color. Start at the top of the leaf line and pull that stroke as long as you can. I used the small end of the MJ Wax Design Tool #2 for big petals on my fern leaves. Start at the right side of the first stroke, down a little, and pull the stroke toward the line. Meet up with the other stroke at the bottom. Pull until you run out

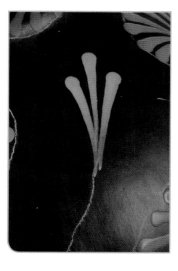

of wax. This stroke is not curved. Start on the left side of the first stroke, down a little, and pull the stroke to the line. This stroke does not have much of a curve to it. Again pull the stroke until you run out of wax.

11.

When it becomes difficult to continue making petals down a leaf at the current angle, stop and turn your gourd upside down or sideways to make the strokes near the bottom. Move the gourd to work for you. It is easier if you pull the strokes toward you.

10.

Now pick a side of the leaf and continue to pull strokes one after another. Make them long enough that they fill in the area. Do not make them so close that they run together.

On the leaf in this picture, I should have made the strokes at the top a little shorter to give the top a slightly sharper point. Start the strokes on the left side until you have caught up with the strokes on the right side. See how the strokes move around the flower on the left? Curved lines will give the leaf a feeling of movement. It looks like that part is moving forward.

When you are making petals in an open area, make sure that you are allowing adequate space for the petals from the other leaf that will to be placed next to it.

12.

This second leaf has a little more curve. Starting at the right of the line, beginning at the top, pull the first stroke down to the center line. Continue to pull the strokes down the right side of the leaf. The ones near the bottom curve a little more.

Repeat with the petals on the left side. Move the petals around the flower and stop when you reach the other leaf. The petals on the right side of this leaf have more curve than those on the left side of this leaf. Notice how to make movement in the leaf. Don't worry about the small black area; you will fill that in later.

13.

Move the gourd to the other section and create a leaf, such as the one shown. You will again start up at the top, where it meets up with the previous leaf. Continue to work your way down the leaf.

Make sure that the top of the fern leaf is always smaller than the bottom of the leaf. You can have the petals be shorter and closer in the middle to show movement of the leaf. Keep the leaves in proportion throughout the gourd.

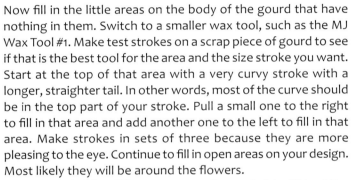

14.

In this next area, a lower leaf is brought in from the side and under the flower, with another leaf starting at the neck of the gourd and stopping when it gets to the lower leaf.

15.

This area is simple. Bring one leaf around each side of the flower. Bring a small fern leaf down under the flower. This should just about fill up the entire gourd. You may do yours differently, but now you

have an idea of how to work the fern leaves around the flowers in different ways.

17.

Now fill in the little areas on the body of the gourd that have nothing in them. Switch to a smaller wax tool, such as the MJ Wax Tool #1. Make test strokes on a scrap piece of gourd to see if that is the best tool for the area and the size stroke you want. Start at the top of that area with a very curvy stroke with a longer, straighter tail. In other words, most of the curve should be in the top part of your stroke. Pull a small one to the right to fill in that area and add another one to the left to fill in that area. Make strokes in sets of three because they are more pleasing to the eye. Continue to fill in open areas on your design. Most likely they will be around the flowers.

You probably will have some small areas left to fill in at the neck of the gourd. You can fill this area with little fern leaves coming down, with some curly strokes as well. Check to see if you have all the little open areas filled. I suggest that you get up and walk away from your gourd for a few minutes, then come back and check it. As we know, sometimes we are too close to a project to see it.

16.

If your gourd is anything like the bottle gourd shown in these photos, you are not done with the top. Gourds with full or partial tops need to be decorated all the way up. If the top has been cut and you plan to add a treatment to the rim, make sure the design is away from the holes in the top of the gourd. Draw lines coming out from the flowers on the top. **Again, keep it away from the holes on top.** Draw a line out from the flower. Make sure to allow room if you have two leaves in that area.

Apply the leaves on the top of the gourd just like you did the other leaves. Consider changing to a smaller wax tool. You may want to practice on a scrap piece of gourd to see what size tool will work best.

When doing two leaves in the same area, make sure to allow room for both. You can also pull a little leaf from the bottom of the flower down into the top part of the gourd to fill in space.

18.

Your next color is Dandelion. This is the color that makes your artwork "pop." I use this color in my artwork as much as I can. A little pop of color can make a huge impact. With the #2 wax tool, add descending dots to the center of your flowers. Keep the dots spaced apart because warm wax dots placed too close can run and lose the dot shape. Allow room in between the yellow dots for the next color. Add centers to all of the flowers.

Change to an orange crayon. Add descending dots to the center of the flowers, but don't overdo it. Make sure you have as much Dandelion showing as orange. Keep the dots far enough apart so that they do not run together. Keep this color plugged in, because you are going to use it one more time.

19.

Using a damp Mr. Clean Magic Eraser, lightly wipe to remove all of the white charcoal pencil lines. Next take a damp paper towel and remove the chalky film left behind by the sponge.

Using the black acrylic paint that you base-coated your gourd with, touch up any scrapes, scratches, or mistakes that you made while working on the gourd. You can also use the paint to cover up any stubborn white lines left behind from the white charcoal pencil. Use a liner brush to get into tight areas. This makes your design clean and crisp again.

20.

Back to your orange wax. Apply dots to those areas that still need a little something to fill them in. Bigger areas may need three descending dots. Do this after clean-up painting because it is easier to paint areas before dots are applied.

Varnish the gourd. Use a brush-on or spray varnish of your choice.

Simple Shell Rim

I found a strand of little shells that really went well with this design. The strand of shells was tight and on a nice string, so I did not need to restring the shells. You'll need a strand of beads, shells, stones, etc. that will reach all the way around the top, and that has at least a 4" to 5" tail of thread that you can tie onto the gourd. Restring them if the string appears weak, or if it doesn't have a long enough tail.

1.

I am using black sinew (to blend the stitches with the base color) to sew the shells onto the rim. You could also use black waxed linen. Use a least three feet of it threaded on an embroidery needle. Start with the needle on the inside in the back and push it through to the front. Pull it over the top of the rim, catching the beginning of the strand of shells. You are not tying into the shell strand. It will be glued and tucked in later. Meet up with the tail in the back and tie a tight knot, but do not cut the tails because you will be using them to tie onto at the end.

2.

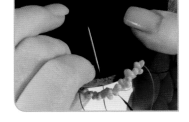

Create a blanket stitch by using your finger to hold the sinew to the left of the next hole on the inside. Take the needle and go through the front of the next hole and catch the sinew on the inside.
This stitch gives you a straight up-and-down line on the front and ties your shells onto the gourd.

3.

Pull the sinew nice and tight, and put it in between your shells. The shells should be close enough that you cannot see space between them.

4.

Continue with this stitch all the way around the top of the gourd. Try to keep the front stitch straight. You can see what the inside of the stitch should look like.

5.

Complete your last stitch at the end of the rim. Take the tail from the beginning of the shell strand and lay it along the top of the rim. Tuck the tail under at least one of the stitches. Trim off the rest of the tail on the shell strand. Glue down the tail with superglue to keep it in place. Allow to dry.

9.

Tuck the end of the shell thread under the other side of the rim. Cut off any extra thread. Superglue the tail down to keep in place.

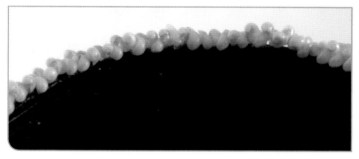

6.

Measure out the remaining shells to have the exact amount needed to cover the top rim of the gourd. Try to get it as exact as you can; you don't want too many or not enough. Remove any extra shells and tie a knot as close to the shell as possible. Cut the thread leaving at least a 3" tail. Put a dot of superglue on the knot so that it cannot come undone. Allow it to dry before touching anything. Do not cut the tail yet.

10.

This is an inside view of the rim and stitches. It should be nice and clean looking. Now that you have learned this simple rim, think about applying it to other gourd projects. Once you have mastered it, it will be a very quick and effective rim to do.

7.

Finish the last stitch, meeting up with the first stitch. Tie the two tails together. Tie a double knot.

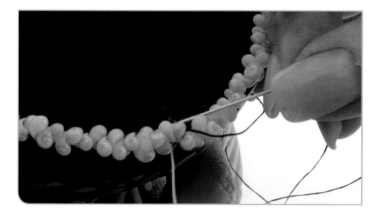

8.

Thread the tails onto the needle and run them back under the shells so they do not show. You can do them both at the same time or you can do them separately and in different directions. Cut off any excess tails.

You have just completed your "Flowers in the Jungle" gourd. What would you do differently next time? Do you like it better without a rim? Would you like the look of a different rim?

Chapter 6
Horsehair Pottery and Turquoise Stone

✓ Supply List

- □ —Bottle gourd, cut and cleaned (exterior cleaned and lightly sanded, cut edge smooth); interior painted
- □ —MJ Wax Liner
- □ —MJ Wax Brush
- □ —one or more wax melting pots
- □ —Mini Oval Craft Template
- □ —Flex-e Ruler
- □ —MJ Texture Brush
- □ —MJ Dry Board
- □ —tray
- □ —drill or Dremel
- □ —5/16" (7.9 mm) round carving bur
- □ —jigsaw or gourd saw
- □ —embossing tool/heat gun
- □ —gourd compass
- □ —Staybowlizer
- □ —Crayola crayons in colors Black, Brown, Robin's Egg, White, and Copper
- □ —acrylic paint (black, ecru, medium gray, tan, and burnt umber)
- □ —black spray paint
- □ —varnish
- □ —Mod Podge Dimensional Magic

- □ —E6000
- □ —tacky glue
- □ —8mm silver colored beads
- □ —½ sequin pins
- □ —awl or bead reamer
- □ —craft or jewelry hammer
- □ —wire cutters
- □ —embroidery needle
- □ —thimble with cross ridges
- □ —superglue
- □ —paintbrush
- □ —fan brush
- □ —craft sponge
- □ —paper plate
- □ —plastic wrap
- □ —scissors
- □ —hobby knife
- □ —white charcoal pencil
- □ —Mr. Clean Magic Eraser
- □ —cotton balls
- □ —Q-tips
- □ —paper towels
- □ —water container

Preparing the Gourd

For this project I used a bottle gourd. Bottle gourds are my favorite. I like the shape and use them in lots of my projects. The shape of this gourd works really well for this design and shows off the stone.

Make sure that the gourd is not too thin. You need the rim to be thick enough that you can put some pins in it, and the sides to be thick enough for some light carving. It does not have to be really thick; medium-thick will work well.

Clean the outside of the gourd. Mark a line around the top of the gourd with a gourd compass. Leave whatever portion of the top section you think will be in proportion to the bottom section of the gourd. Cut the top with your jigsaw or gourd saw.

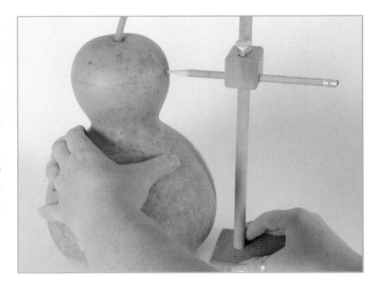

Using the MJ Mini Oval Craft Templates find the third template from the center of the templates. The stone area has to be small enough that you can contain all of the melted wax, but large enough to show the stone. I wouldn't go bigger than 2½" to 3" long. You could do a round shape if you like that better.

Find the middle in the bottom part of your gourd—the area that is flattest. Hold the template on and in place by placing a finger on top and one finger on the bottom. Line the template up, making sure it is straight. With your white charcoal pencil, trace the template on the inside of the oval.

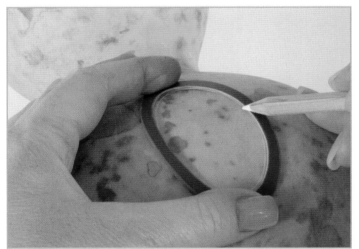

Remember to carve in a well-ventilated area with your face mask on. The size of the round carving bur depends on the size of the beads you are using. I used a ⁵⁄₁₆" (7.9 mm) round carving bur because I am using an 8-mm bead. In other words, you want the bur to be the same size as the beads. Attach the bit to your drill or Dremel. Place the bit so it lines up with the white line right in the center of the bit. Carve along the drawn line by carefully and evenly pulling the bit toward you as you go around the oval. Turn the gourd as you go around the oval so that you continue to pull the bit toward you. The groove should not be too deep but deep enough to hold the beads in place. The groove does not have to be perfect. Make it only as wide as the carving bur, no wider. Go around the oval and meet up where you started.

Sponging on Texture

1.

Wet a craft sponge (not sea sponge), wringing it out really well. Pour a small amount of an off-white acrylic paint, such as Linen from Folk Art or Sandstone from Delta, onto a paper plate. Pick up the paint with your damp sponge, and apply it to the gourd by dabbing it on. This puts a thick layer of paint on the gourd and gives it a sandy look. By starting on the bottom you will get the hang of dabbing it on before moving to the main body of the gourd. That will also help the bottom to dry first so that you can place the gourd on its bottom while the rest of it dries.

Sponge around, not on, the stone. It is okay if you get a little paint on the stone area, but don't paint it.

2.

Sponge paint onto the rest of the gourd. You may have to really press the sponge to get paint in the neck area of the gourd. Allow to dry. You can apply a second layer if your first layer is thin. It is okay if some of the gourd color shows through. You will be putting many layers of paint on the gourd but the goal is for it to look natural.

3.

On this project, I'm going to show you several ways to "sponge" on paint. Each way results in a slightly different texture. The first way is by using plastic wrap. Using a 12" piece of plastic wrap, scrunch it up in your hand, but don't wad it up into a ball. It should be kind of loose, and should fit in the palm of your hand.

4.

Pour a small amount of medium gray paint onto a paper plate. You do not want a dark gray. The color I used was Rain Gray by Delta. With the plastic wrap, pull the paint out to the side from the paint puddle. **This is very important.** It keeps you from getting a glob of paint on your gourd. Now "pounce" the plastic wrap in the area of paint you pulled out, not in the middle of the puddle of paint.

5.

Always start at the bottom of the gourd. This way, if you get a glob of paint, it will be at the bottom where no one can see it. Pounce the plastic wrap various places around the gourd, like you would do in marbleizing. Start from the bottom and come partway up, but not in straight lines. Have some branch off in a second line. Make sure that you have some on the top and neck of the gourd.

Start some lines of gray at the middle of the gourd near the carved area. Bring it halfway or more around the stone. Don't overdo it now; you can always add more later. Reload if you run out of paint.

You should not have a solid gray color. Only about one-third of the gourd should have gray on it, and the rest of the area should be the basecoat color. This allows you to see a design.

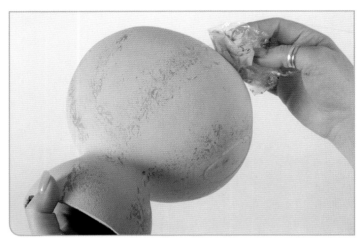

9.

If you feel there is too much paint in an area, use scrunched-up plastic wrap to pounce the base color over the dark area until you lighten it up. You can do this on any area of the gourd you feel is too dark.

6.

With the plastic wrap loaded with your basecoat color, lightly go back over the gray areas you just did. This sets the gray color down into the base color and helps makes it look more natural.

7.

If you feel you need a little more gray, use the MJ Wax Texture Brush and apply gray to those areas again. The texture brush will give it a lighter texture and helps it appear more natural. When loading paint into the texture brush, pull the paint off to the side of the plate (out of the puddle of paint) and pounce into this area with the texture brush. This avoids having too much paint on the brush.

10.

Pour out a puddle of white acrylic paint, and use the plastic wrap as before. Apply white paint here and there on the gourd over the open areas, as well as on top of the gray line areas. Do not apply too much. This is just one more element that really gives it that rock feel.

8.

Wash the gray paint from your texture brush using soap and water; dry it. Repeat the previous step with Burnt Umber acrylic paint. This color applied with the texture brush is going to help give the gourd a grainier, sandy feel. Pounce over the same area you have been working on. Try to keep the darker color a little more inside the gray area to give it more of a burnt look.

11.

Using black acrylic paint, paint the rim of the gourd. If you painted it earlier you'll need to touch it up. Make sure you keep the paint off the front of the gourd.

Paint the carved area around the stone. You may have to touch this area up again, but it's easier to do it now and touch it up later.

12.

Dip a fan brush into water and then into a little puddle of black paint. This will water down the black paint. Now take a second brush and hit the fan brush in the middle to create black specks or little dots. Be careful about where the paint is going; the speckles will fly everywhere. You may want to practice on a gourd scrap until you're happy with the results. Move the fan brush around until you get the entire gourd. You may have to reload the fan brush.

How to Make a Stone Using Wax

Now you are going to take everything you've learned about wax design and throw it out the window... well, maybe not throw it out, but put it aside until the next project. You are going to use wax in a totally different way. The method I use to make the stone I call "twice melted."

1.

Start by warming up the melting pot and adding Robin's Egg for the turquoise color. (You can also make turquoise by using equal parts of blue-green and white, mixing the colors together well until they become one solid color.) Using your embossing gun, heat the stone section of the gourd until it is warm. This will help the wax go on smoothly.

Dip your MJ Wax Brush into the turquoise wax and start to brush it onto the stone area. Try to keep the wax as smooth as possible. Do not go over the wax while it is cooling, since that just makes the wax rough. If the wax runs out or is no longer smooth, place your brush back into the wax and reload. Let the first coat cool off.

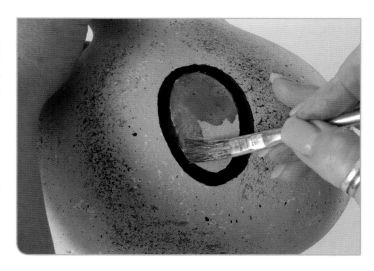

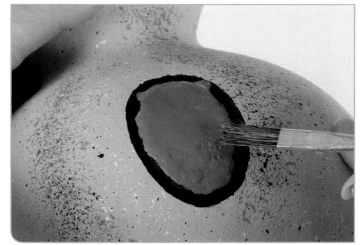

2.

Once the first layer is cool, apply a second layer of wax. It may be a little harder to keep the wax as smooth in this layer.

45

3.

Add black to a melting pot. Once the black crayon is melted, set your hobby knife in the wax to get it warm. You are going to use the hobby knife as a painting tool. You'll create the lines in the stone, which makes it look more natural. Pull the knife up the side of the well to take off most of the wax. Go to the stone, and draw marble lines. Try not to cut into the turquoise wax. You want to just draw thin lines on with the wax. Pull until the blade runs out of wax and reload. Heat the hobby knife again and move onto the next line. Split some of the lines. Don't overdo it—just a couple of lines are fine.

4.

You can put white in a melting pot, or you can cheat a little by taking the white crayon and rubbing it on the top corner of a warm melting pot. This will give you enough white for this step. Take a Q-tip and pick up the white wax, and dab it here and there on your stone. Again, less is better.

5.

With your embossing gun, start heating around the outside of the stone first, then the whole stone. You will see it turn shiny. That means the wax is melting. You do not want to overheat the wax; move the embossing tool farther away to heat it less, or closer to heat it more. You might want to practice on a scrap piece of gourd. This happens fast—it is all done in under a minute.

The entire stone should be melted. The lines and white on the stone will start to move around; however, you don't want it to move too much. Heat it until you like the design in the stone. If you do not like the design, get a paper towel and, while the wax is still warm, wipe it off, trying to keep the stone wax off the rest of the gourd. Create the stone again until you are happy with it. You will find out that when it comes to heating the stone, less heating time is better.

While the wax is still warm, use a Q-tip to remove any wax that got into the carved part on the sides. You can use your hobby knife if needed.

6.

Put copper-colored wax into your melting pot. Take a new wax brush (the wax brushes are hard to get clean so I just keep one for each color) and dip the wax brush into the well to pick up the color. Rub the brush on top of your finger to sprinkle copper dots on the stone. Stay close to the stone. You don't want copper dots on the rest of your gourd.

Your stone is completed! Now you can create your own wax stones instead of buying them.

Touch up any paint around the edge of the stone with your black acrylic paint.

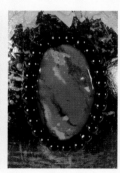

You can change the stone just by changing the color of the wax. The base color of the first stone is Dandelion crayon with red and black lines. The black stone is done with white lines and white wax dabbed on with the Q-tip. Red crayon is used for this stone with black, white, and gold lines. Notice for this stone I used black beads instead of silver ones for a different look. How about a green or purple stone? The possibilities are unlimited.

How to Use the Wax Liner

Put brown crayon into your melting pot. It's better to put this color in ahead of time and let it get really warm. That helps to thin down the wax and makes it easier to use with the MJ Wax Liner. Set the liner into the wax and let it heat up, too. Make sure you leave it in for a minute or more. Brown crayons are a little thicker and sometimes it is harder to get brown wax to flow through the liner. The more you heat the wax and the longer you heat the liner, the better it will work.

Once the liner is warm and the wax is hot and thin, scoop up the brown wax into the well of the wax liner.

1.

Keep the tool upright on the gourd. Start to add lines in the gray sections of the gourd. When you first set the liner down, the wax lines may be a little heavier. If that bothers you, keep a paper towel next to the area you are working on and wipe the liner on the paper towel first, and then onto your project.

These lines are meant to look like horsehair in horsehair pottery. The lines are usually in little clusters. Make sure to twist and turn the lines; they should not be straight. (Look up horsehair pottery on the Internet to see what it looks like.) It is better to have too few than too many. Make sure to bring some lines to the outside of the gray areas.

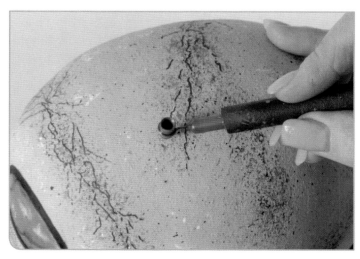

2.

Now add one more layer of texture to the gourd. Use medium brown acrylic paint with a craft sponge and lightly pounce the last layer of texture over the gray areas. Apply some outside the gray areas. Keep it very light. Start at the bottom of the gourd to make sure your color will be light enough in the main area of the gourd.

In the style of pottery that's the inspiration for this project, horsehair is applied to the pottery and then it is fired. The horsehair burns off, leaving the burn marks of the horsehair. The medium brown you apply helps achieve that look.

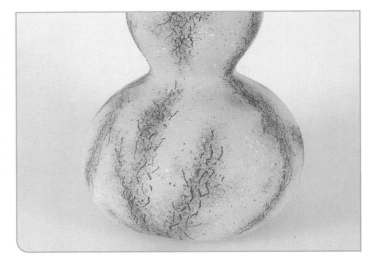

3.

To clean your wax liner, wipe the outside of the liner while it is still warm. Dump out any remaining wax in the well of the liner. Take a Q-tip and push out any wax still in the well. Use the other end of the Q-tip to clean the inside of the well. Clean out your melting pot and add black crayon. Black crayon is thinner than the brown, and it will flow out of the liner faster and spread wider. Add just a little to the gray areas.

Keep the black lines in the middle of the gray areas only. That is where the thickest horsehair would be. Less is more!

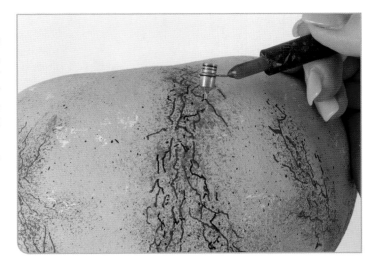

4.

To give the feel of the horsehair being burned out of the pottery, you are going to heat the wax with the embossing gun just a little. If you like the way your gourd looks now you can skip this part. You can do a test sample of the bottom of the gourd to see if you like it. Lightly heat the wax lines until they turn shiny. Careful! Do not overheat the wax.

Keep the embossing gun moving. It's better to heat a little and then reheat, than to overheat it. Be careful while heating around the stone. Try not to heat it. I put a piece of cardboard or paper in front of the stone to shield it from heat.

Choose your favorite spray varnish or brush-on varnish. Apply and let dry. You will be finishing the stone later but it's okay if you varnish it now too.

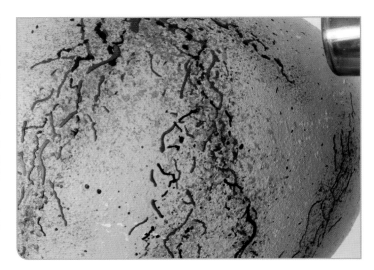

How to Bead the Rim

I developed a method of putting beads on a gourd rim without drilled holes being visible. I use a similar method on my jewelry. You need to make sure that the gourd rim is thick enough for a pin to go into it without splitting your gourd. For the rim, you'll use sequin pins or appliqué pins that are ½" long. It is important that the pins are not longer. (I tried this method with all kinds of pins and little nails. The other items cracked the gourd or I was unable to get them into the rim.) Sequin pins can be found in the pin section of the craft store.

It is better to have a gourd with sides that are straight up and down in the area of the rim, or with as little curve as possible. If your gourd curves too much, the pins may poke out.

1.

This next step is so important. Without it, the pins won't go in. Take a bead reamer or thin awl and poke it straight down, in the center of the rim, to a depth of ¼". No farther or the pin will not stay in. If your gourd top is slanted, you want to follow the direction of the gourd. Make sure, if the pin will poke out due to the curve, that it goes through the inside of the gourd, not the front.

2.

Place a sequin pin in the hole you just made. You will have half of the pin left.

3.

Place the thimble on your finger and push the sequin straight down into the gourd. Leave the pin sticking up just enough to wrap the sinew around it. (Don't try to hammer the sequin in—it will only bend the sequin. Trust me, I have lots of experience.)

Your thimble should have cross ridges on it. This way the pin will not slide around on the thimble.

4.

Take a piece of sinew. If your sinew is thick, split it into 2 or 3 sections. I use sinew because it is strong and the wax helps hold the thread in place without slipping as much. Tie the sinew onto the pin with a double knot, leaving at least a 5" tail.

5.

With the edge of the thimble, push the pin the rest of the way into the gourd. It works so much better if you are using the edge of the thimble instead of the middle. The first time you do this it seems hard but it will get easier and easier as you proceed. You might want to practice on a scrap piece of gourd.

6.

Insert your second pin about ⅓" from the first one. The more the rim curves around, the closer the pins need to be. Conversely, the straighter the area the farther apart the pins can be. Basically, the pins can be between ¼" and ½" apart.

Leave the pin sticking up enough that you can wrap the sinew around it. Wrap the thread clockwise around the pin. Keep it nice and tight. Make sure to always wrap in the same direction.

7.

Push the pin all the way in with the edge of the thimble. Make sure that it is flush with the rim. If you cannot get the pin in the last little bit of the way, you can use a craft hammer or jewelry hammer to lightly tap the pin in. (Using the hammer when the pin is not almost all the way in will only bend the pin.)

The more slowly you push in the pin, the less it is likely to bend. If you bend a pin, pull it out with your pliers. It is not worth the time or hassle to try and straighten it out.

8.

Continue to work around the rim. Remember to always wrap the sinew around the pin in the same direction.

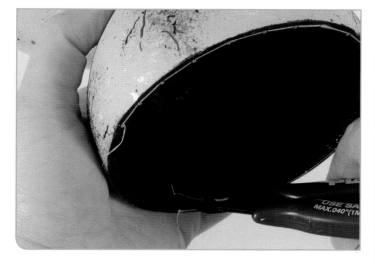

9.

If you have a pin poke through the front, stop before you do any further damage to the paint. Pull the pin out. Start a new hole and try again. If the pin comes through the inside of the gourd and the pin is in securely enough, take the wire cutters and cut off the pin point that is poking out.

Try to cut it as flush as you can to the gourd so no wire is showing. Put a dot of tacky glue over where the pin came out. Just a small dot over the metal keeps it from catching on the thread or poking anyone. You can paint the glue black once it's dry so that it does not show.

If you have a soft gourd and the pins come out of the gourd, put a little superglue on the pins to hold them in place. Out of all the gourds I've done, this has happened only once. But sometimes you may have just one pin, or pins in a certain area on the rim, that won't stay in.

10.

Once you've gone all the way around the rim, tie the tail to the current thread, tightly so that you have no slack. The knot should be at the first pin you did on the rim. Do not cut the threads.

11.

Add a needle that will fit through your beads onto the longest length of the sinew. Thread two beads onto the needle. I used 8-mm metal silver beads rather than real silver or silver plate beads that will tarnish. I would not use smaller than 6-mm beads when beading on a rim, since the beads need to be big enough to cover up the rim. (To make it easy for you the beads are available at www.miriamjoy.com.)

This is the only time you will thread more than one bead on at a time. Slide the beads onto the thread. Adjust them nice and tight up to the knot and the first pin.

Hold the sinew with your left hand to keep it out of the way. Take your needle and go under the thread that you pinned onto the rim, next to the last bead toward the inside of the gourd. You are working toward your left. Make sure that you are always working and adding beads to the left.

12.

Continue to hold the sinew with your left hand to keep it out of the way. Take the needle and go behind the last bead and push the needle through the bead. Pull the thread.

13.

Add another bead onto the thread. Move that bead down, right next to the last bead. Remember you are adding beads and working to the left. Take your needle and go under the thread on the

rim, right in front of the last bead you added. Pull the thread through. Sometimes you may have to move where you pull the needle through a little to the left or right if the pin is in the way. Pull the thread tight but not too tight.

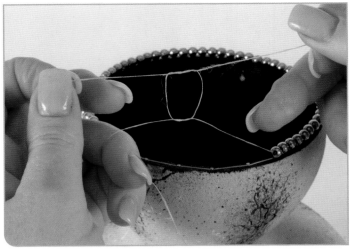

15.

Eventually you will run out of sinew. Stop when you have at least a 5" tail. Take another piece of sinew and add that piece on with a double knot. The beads you are using have a hole large enough that the knot will go through the beads.

14.

Hold the sinew with your left hand to keep it out of the way. Again pass the thread behind the last bead and through the bead. Pull the thread through. The beads should start to lie nice and even. If you have a bead that does not lay nicely or starts to bunch up, take the bead or beads off and redo that part. Most likely you just have the thread crossed or the thread went through the bead in the wrong direction. That is why it is so important to remember that you are working to the left.

Add another bead and push it down till it is next to the other beads. Continue this process all the way around the rim.

16.

Leave the tails long; cut the frayed ends off and thread them into the needle. If you can't get both tails into the eye of the needle together you can do them one at a time. Take the needle and slide it back through several beads till the needle pops out or you have gone a couple of inches. Pull the thread out of the beads.

Cut the thread off as close to the bead as you can. This keeps the thread from showing. If you happen to be using a slick or plastic thread, you may want to superglue your knots to keep them from slipping. I put the superglue on my needle then onto the knot. This is how I keep from making a mess with the glue or gluing the beads down.

17.

Once you have finished all the way around the rim, you have to decide if you have room for the last bead or not. String the last bead, and if the beads do not lie in a straight line and start to bunch up, do not add that bead. When you tie the end of the area, the beads will even out and will fill in.

18.

If you have room, go ahead and add the last bead. With your needle, come from behind the last bead and go through the first bead you did on the rim. Pull the string through the beads.

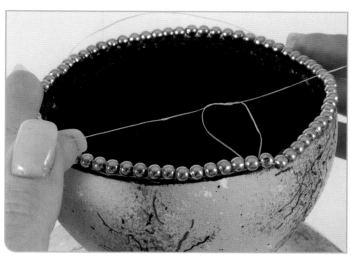

19.

Pick up the tail of the thread from when you started the beading. Tie it to the thread you have now. Do a double knot. Make sure that you have it nice and tight. Keep your needle on your thread.

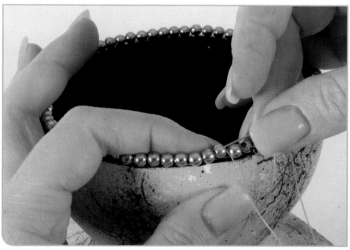

20.

Start with the beads closest to the knot. Push your needle through the beads for a couple of inches to hide the thread. Pull the thread out nice and tight. Cut the thread right next to the bead so the thread does not show. This finishes your rim. What other project can you see doing this rim on? It is amazing that a simple rim can add so much.

21.

When is the best time to add the shine to the stone? You could do this step before you do the beading on the rim; in that case, you'd have to wait to do the rim so the stone can dry/cure overnight. Instead, adding the high shine at this later point in the process allows you to finish the rest of the gourd without waiting for the stone to dry and cure.

Use Mod Podge Dimensional Magic on the stone. It is important that it is Dimensional Magic and not a regular Mod Podge product. It gives the stone a dimension and makes it look like a polished stone. It is the thickest product out there right now and is used to add dimension to paper and jewelry.

Do not shake the bottle; it adds bubbles, which you do not want. If you happen to get a bubble, pop it with a pin. Start on the outside of the stone, just enough that it covers all of the wax completely but does not run down into the carved part of the stone. Go completely around the stone. Keeping in a circular motion, slowly start to fill in the center. Stop periodically and allow it to spread out a little and continue in a circular motion until you reach the center. Stopping and letting the liquid spread out a bit, keeps you from adding too much varnish and starting to flow over the sides of the stone and into the carved area. The liquid should still be very thick on the stone. If some of the liquid starts to overflow, take a Q-tip and remove it.

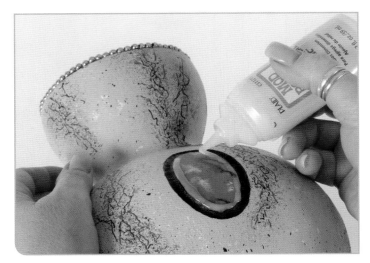

22.

You can also use your embossing gun and lightly blow heat onto the stone until a film forms on top to help keep the liquid in place. Place the gourd on its side so the stone is as level as possible while it dries. It will take several hours to dry. I try to time it so that I can allow it to dry overnight.

How to Bead Around the Stone

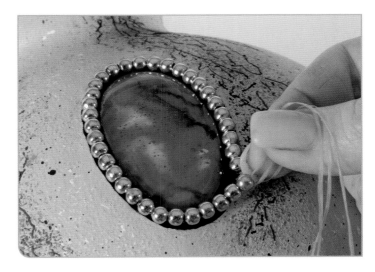

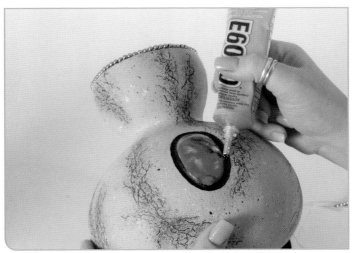

1.

Take a thread (any kind will do) and string your beads. Use the same 8-mm beads that were used to determine the size of the carved channel. Put enough beads onto the thread to go completely around the stone. Do not tie the thread anywhere.

2.

Use E6000 to glue the beads on. E6000 is very strong glue that works on hard-to-glue items. Put glue around the stone in the carved area but not so much that you have glue coming out the edges when you put the beads in.

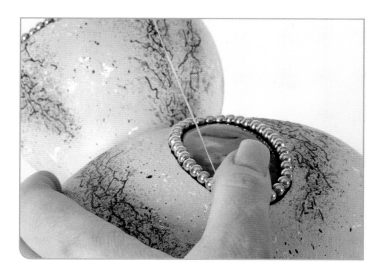

3.

Keeping the strung beads tight, start to lay them on the glue. Do not let the beads turn so the glue is on top. Lay them completely around all of the stone. Hold the last few beads down with your thumb where the string is coming out. Pull the string slowly out of the beads. There will be no thread or string remaining in the beads. It is just used to get the beads in place. If there is room for the last bead without it being too tight, put it in. If the beads start to buckle, take that bead out and just move the beads a little to adjust for that area.

Place the gourd back on its side with the stone level so the glue can dry. If you sit the gourd up, the beads will slide and fall off. Allow a few hours to dry.

Now you have an embedded stone that has beads around it with half the work. It looks like you spent a pretty penny on the stone.

There were so many useful techniques in this project. You learned how to sponge texture in lots of different ways, including using the texture brush. We covered how to use the wax liner and how to apply the wax with a brush, as well as slightly melting it for a burned (melted) look. Along with learning how to make stones out of wax, you learned how to bead on the rim without drill holes, and how to add beads around the stone.

I would like to thank the person who was the inspiration behind this gourd: Sherry Briscoe. Sherry is a wonderful teacher and a great friend. I had the privilege of spending some time with Sherry and we taught each other some gourd projects. Being a Southwest artist, I was drawn to her "End of Trails" gourd, and she taught me how to make it. I told Sherry, "I think I have a way of doing this in wax," and she gave me permission to teach my version of the gourd.

With great teachers comes great inspiration. If you ever have a chance to take a class from this wonderful teacher, do not pass it up. Thank you, Sherry and Bob, for all you do for the gourd world. God bless.

Chapter 7
Midnight Ferns with Crocheted Ruffled Rim

✓ Supply List

- ☐ —Round gourd, cut and cleaned (exterior cleaned and lightly sanded, cut edge smooth); interior painted; exterior base-coated with two coats of black acrylic paint
- ☐ —MJ Wax Design Tool #0
- ☐ —MJ Wax Design Tool #00
- ☐ —one or more wax melting pots
- ☐ —MJ Circle Craft Templates
- ☐ —MJ Mini Square Craft Template
- ☐ —Flex-e Ruler
- ☐ —MJ Dry Board
- ☐ —tray
- ☐ —drill and drill bit
- ☐ —jigsaw or gourd saw
- ☐ —gourd compass
- ☐ —Staybowlizer
- ☐ —Crayola crayons in colors Dandelion, Orange, and White (3 White crayons needed)
- ☐ —black acrylic paint
- ☐ —black spray paint
- ☐ —varnish
- ☐ —white crochet thread size 5 size
- ☐ —D crochet hook
- ☐ —size 6/0 E-black iridescent beads
- ☐ —embroidery needle
- ☐ —paintbrush
- ☐ —scissors
- ☐ —hobby knife
- ☐ —white charcoal pencil
- ☐ —Mr. Clean Magic Eraser
- ☐ —cotton balls
- ☐ —Q-tips
- ☐ —paper towels
- ☐ —water container

Preparing the Gourd

For this project you can use any type of round gourd. Cut the top with your jigsaw or gourd saw. Clean out the inside of the gourd. Sand the blemishes and scratches off the outside of the gourd.

Sand the rim of the gourd smooth so the embroidery thread does not get caught in it. The rim should also be flat.

Lightly sand the inside edge of the rim. This helps to keep the embroidery thread from getting caught.

You are going to be using size 5 crochet thread for this project and a size D crochet hook. Choose a drill bit that is large enough for your D crochet hook to fit through the holes easily. I can't specify a bit size for you, because crochet hooks are different shapes. The hooks are usually wider in the middle; the middle of the hook does not have to fit through the hole.

Use a Flex-e to measure your rim.

Drill the holes ½" down from the top of the rim. Space the holes ½" apart from each other. Use an air compressor or canned air to blow out the gourd dust that results from the drilling.

Basecoat the outside of the gourd with two coats of black acrylic paint. Varnish the gourd with one coat of varnish at this time to keep the gourd clean and protected. It can be spray or brush-on. If you were doing any design other than a wax design, you would finish the project and varnish it and then do the rim. But because the wax is softer, you are going to do the rim first and then apply the wax last. This also helps keep the black on the gourd cleaner.

Crocheted Ruffled Rim

You will be using a size 5 crochet thread. If you wanted the ruffles to be stiffer, you could use a thicker thread. There are lots of wonderful YouTube videos to help you understand the stitch types and how to crochet each stitch.

1.

Pull your thread through one of the holes in the gourd rim. Tie the thread tightly using a double knot to keep it in place. You can lay the tail on the rim to your left to crochet over the top of it, or weave it in later.

2.

Wrap your crochet thread around your left forefinger and keep it taut. Holding the crochet hook in your right hand, insert it under the crochet thread at the front of the gourd, and grab the thread with the crochet hook.

3.

Pull the thread forward and through to form a slip stitch on the hook.

4.

Chain two. A chain is when you put thread over your crochet hook and pull it through the loop already on your hook. This counts as one double crochet. Loop the crochet thread around the hook.

5.

Insert the crochet hook through the same hole in front. Grab the thread with the crochet hook on the inside of the gourd. Pull it back through to the front.

6.

Move the thread around so that it is on the top of the rim. Wrap your crochet thread around the hook and pull it through the first two loops.

7.

Wrap your crochet thread around the hook and pull through both loops, forming a double crochet.

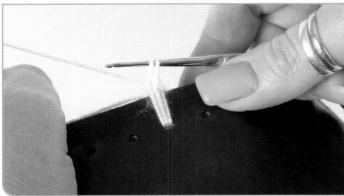

8.

You should end up with one single loop. Wrap the crochet thread around the hook. Insert the hook through the front hole for the second time, same hole as the last time. Wrap the thread around the hook and pull it back through the front of the gourd. Pull the thread up to the top of the rim. Wrap the thread around the crochet hook and pull through the first two loops. Wrap the thread around the crochet hook and pull through the last two loops forming another double crochet. This will give you a total of three double crochets in this hole.

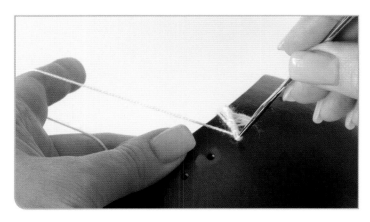

9.

Wrap the thread around your crochet hook. Insert the crochet hook into the next hole. Have no worries if your threads do not look neat in the beginning of a stitch. This picture shows you that mine is not "neat" either. Inside the gourd, wrap the thread around the crochet hook and pull through the same hole to the front.

10.

Move the thread to the top of the rim.

11.

Wrap the thread around your crochet hook. Pull through the first two loops.

12.

Wrap your thread around the crochet hook and pull it through the last two hoops. Do two more double crochets in this hole.

13.

Continue around the rim making sure each hole has three double crochet stitches in it. You should see six threads in each hole.

14.

Complete the last three double crochet stitches in the last hole on the rim. You will have a loop left on your crochet hook.

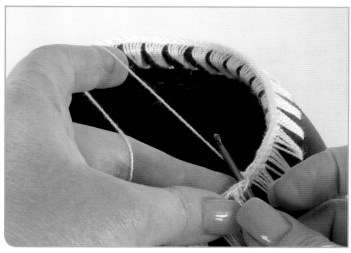

15.

Row 2. Take your crochet hook and go into the top of the first double crochet stitch. Wrap the thread around the top of the crochet hook. Pull the thread through the stitch and through the loop on the crochet hook creating a slip stitch.

16.

Chain three by pulling the thread through the loop on the crochet hook, three times. Counts as one double crochet stitch.

Wrap the thread around the hook and insert it into the top of the next double crochet on the bottom row. Pull the thread through the top of the stitch and two loops. Wrap the thread around the crochet hook and pull it through the last two loops forming a double crochet. Do one more double crochet in the same space, for a total of three double crochet stitches.

18.

Do three double crochets in the top of each stitch on the bottom row. Go completely around the first row until you are at the beginning.

19.

Pull the thread through the first stitch and through the loop on the crochet hook creating a slip stitch to complete that row.

20.

Row 3. Chain three. Add a double crochet in the top of each of the stitches on the previous row. Repeat all the way around the third row until you meet up with the first stitch.

21.

Pull the thread through the top of the first stitch of this row and the loop on your crochet hook to form a slip stitch and complete the third row. You can stop here if you do not want to add beads to your rim.

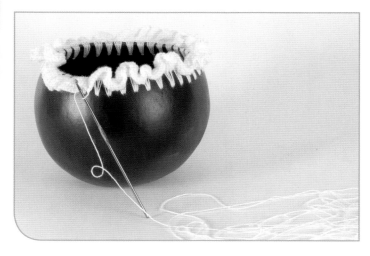

22.

To add beads. Pull lots of thread from the spool. Pull as much as you are comfortable working with. Cut the end off from the spool. You can always tie more thread on later if needed.

23.

Use an embroidery or tapestry needle that is big enough for the crochet thread but not too large for the bead. Use black size 6/0 E-beads or a bead big enough to go over the crochet thread. String as many beads on at a time as you are comfortable working with. For me, it is easier to string more on at the beginning, because there is plenty of room to move them along the extra thread that's been pulled out. Bring the beads up the thread, close to the rim. I leave the needle on so I can string more if needed.

24.

Row 4. Using the crochet hook, chain one, by pulling the thread through the last loop.

25.

Slide one bead down just above the chain you did. Chain one after the bead by pulling the thread through the last loop.

26.

Chain one for a total of three including the one with the bead.

27.

Insert your hook into the top of the next stitch on the last row you just did. Wrap your thread once around the crochet hook and pull it through that stitch and the stitch on your crochet hook to form a slip stitch. Chain three including the one in the middle with the bead.

28.

Continue adding the three chains with a bead in the middle chain to the top stitches from the last row around the entire rim. Once you are comfortable with the stitches you can keep several beads lined up on your thread to make it go faster.

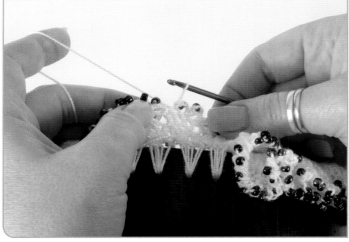

29.

Once you have gone all the way around, do a slip stitch with the first stitch you did on this row. Pull the thread through the last loop to form a knot. Cut the thread off leaving a 2" to 3" tail. Weave the tail back into the ruffle.

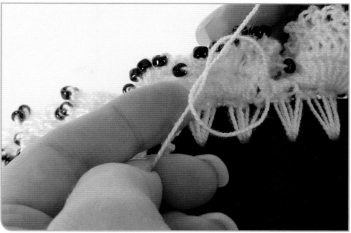

30.

Cut another piece of crochet thread that is three feet long, or longer if you are doing a bigger gourd. Thread it onto your needle. Come up under the ruffle and insert it in the top of the first row next to the gourd rim. You can tie a knot on the end of the thread if you need to. Leave at least a 5" tail.

33.

Once you have completed the entire row, stick your needle down to the underside of the ruffle and pull the thread through. You should be right next to the tail from when you started. Tie a double knot to secure the thread. Shorten the tails to 2" or 3" long. Take your crochet hook and go in and out of the threads under the rim. Pull the tails through with your hook to hide them.

Once you get the hang of it, it's a simple rim. Think of other gourd designs that you could add this ruffled rim to. What other colors of threads or beads would you like to use? I would love to do this with a variegated thread.

31.

You are adding beads next to the rim to help make it more colorful and attractive design. Bring your needle through the top of the ruffle base and through the top of the first stitch.

32.

Add a bead and catch the top of the next stitch. Add another bead and catch the top of the next stitch. You will be adding a bead every other stitch around the top of the rim.

"Midnight Ferns" Wax Design

Let's get ready to put a design on this fun gourd. Tuck all the ruffles inside the gourd to keep them as clean as possible and out of the way.

1.

Start by finding the bottom of the gourd where the gourd rests on its base. With the white charcoal pencil, go around to mark where the gourd meets the table.

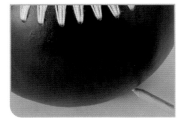

2.

If you are working with a round gourd, you should have a fairly round mark on the bottom of the gourd. You are not going to put wax on this area. This is where you will start your design. Grab your MJ Circle Craft Templates and find the size of circle closest to the circle on the gourd. Lay the template on the gourd and trace the inside of the circle with the white charcoal pencil. Do not go into that circle when applying the pattern.

3.

With the white charcoal pencil, add a swirl from the top. Keep it curved, not a straight line. Go almost all the way to the bottom of the gourd. Curl the line so it is a smaller swirl at the bottom.

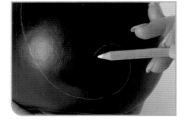

4.

Start another center line swirl from the bottom of the gourd next to the circle. Draw a curved line out, up, and around. Draw the tail into a tighter swirl. Remember when applying the center line to your design to allow room for strokes on both sides of the line to create the fern leaf.

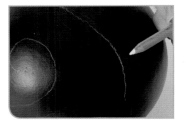

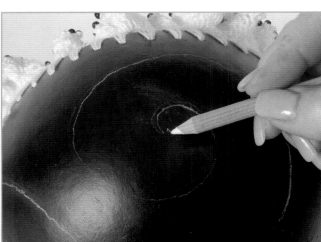

5.

Do a big swirl this time starting at the bottom, and bring it around until it is next to the design on your left. Allow room for both designs to have petals on each side of that line.

6.

From the swirl you just created, draw a short line out a couple of inches up. Make this one a couple of inches long.

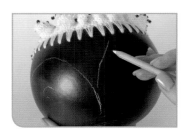

7.

On the next area to the right, do a big swirl going to the right this time. Take up the room from the top to the bottom of the gourd. Allow room for the design on the top and bottom. You may 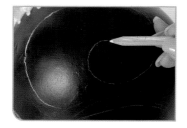 need a couple of more swirls or some more lines branching out from the design if you have a bigger gourd. As long as you have the basic shapes you can always add more later on.

8.

Start heating up your melting pot. For this project you will need two to three crayons, depending on the size of your gourd and on whether you get carried away or not. You will mostly use the MJ Wax Design Tool #0. You can also use the smaller tool #00 if you need smaller strokes.

Remember that white needs to be stirred a little more. Stir the white when it separates from the wax. White can also drip a little more. You should not have too many drips in this project because you're using a smaller tool. If dripping occurs check to see what is around you that is affecting the wax, such as heat blowing, air conditioners, or fans.

The stroke that you will use on this project is a little different. You are going to lay the tool down on your gourd, pull, and lift to form a little tail. It is not like the long tails where you let the wax run out on its own. You may find that it is easier to add a dot and then pull the tail with the wax tool. Do this all at one time. Do not let the wax cool in between. You may want to practice on a scrap piece of gourd until you are comfortable. Make sure your tool is warm.

Start at the end of the branch outline that you added to the swirl. Pull the stroke in the direction of the line. Pull a stroke on each side of the first one you did. Make sure the two strokes are down just a bit from the first one. With the white charcoal pencil, starting under the strokes you just did, add little branches. The branches should get longer as they go down the middle line. Do not have the branches too close together—leave room for the leaves.

9.

Start with the branches next to the one you just did. Do the first stroke down the middle and one on either side of the first stroke.

10.

Add more strokes if needed to fill in the branch. The strokes get bigger as you work your way down the branch.

11.

Come back to the center line of the branches using the same method with a stroke down the middle and one on each side of it to fill in the open area between the branches.

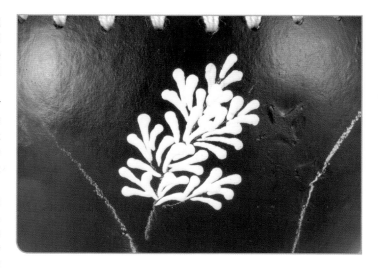

12.

Move on to the next section of little branches. These strokes can be a little longer. Start with the middle stroke and work your way down the branches until you get to the middle line. Using the same method, go back and fill any open area between the branches.

13.

Go back to the top of the leaf and add a few smaller strokes on the top. You do not want these strokes to touch any of the other strokes. Making smaller strokes, pull some from the outside of the design toward it. Do not touch any strokes on the inside design. This will give it more dimension and make it more airy. You can switch to the #00 tool for these strokes if you want them smaller. All of the leaves are going to be done in this same basic manner.

16.

The branches should get a little wider as you continue to work toward the bottom of the leaf. This is done gradually. Make sure you are filling in between the branches.

14.

Move to the inside of a swirl on the left of the design you are working on. Do a couple of strokes, turning them as they are added. Keep the first three strokes one after another all on the same side of the center line. Start adding  your strokes, one down the middle and one to each side of the first stroke. Add more to any side as needed. Start to draw your little branches. Go back in and fill the branches in between.

17.

Have the two designs meet up to create one design. The branches on the bottom will be bigger after the two meet up. Add some smaller strokes to the outside of the branches but not touching them.

15.

Continue adding the little branches and working down around the swirl. Draw them on with a white charcoal pencil.

18.

Move on to the big swirl going to the left. Start this swirl just like you did the last one. Start to add little branches getting bigger as you go. Continue moving down the fern, getting  bigger as you move toward the bottom of the fern. Make sure to fill in areas between the branches.

19.

Above this swirl is an area big enough to draw a branch off another fern. Curve it around the top of the other swirl. Start at the top of the fern in the area you need to fill in. Keep the line curved. No straight-up-and-down ferns. Curves help create the natural feel of the design.

20.

Add smaller ferns to fill in open areas. Start at the top and work down the line creating branches to the bottom. Keep the fern as narrow as you need to fill in the area. You could also do a fern from the bottom to the top. Fill in with smaller strokes around the outside of the leaf. These strokes should not touch the leaf design. Check to see that you have done this to all of the leaves. This also helps fill in open areas that are too small to add a fern.

21.

Take your Mr. Clean Magic Eraser and remove any white lines that are showing. Take a damp paper towel and remove the film left behind from the Magic Eraser. Let it dry.

Touch up any paint that needs touching up at this time with the basecoat color. Paint over any white lines that may still be showing. Don't worry if the paint does not blend in. It will as soon as the gourd is varnished.

Push the ruffled rim up. Put painter's tape around the ruffle to keep from getting varnish on it. Spray or brush on several layers of varnish onto your design.

Black and white gourds are the most popular of my gourds. I use black because it is a background color, meaning it fades into the background, allowing your eyes to see the design. Black and white is so appealing. If you want to sell a gourd, do it in black and white.

Chapter 8
Blue Horizons with Arrowhead Points Rim

✓Supply List

- ☐ —Kettle gourd with smooth, level opening, cut and cleaned (exterior cleaned and lightly sanded, cut edge smooth); interior painted with black spray paint; exterior base-coated with two coats of black acrylic paint
- ☐ —#2 MJ Wax Design Tool
- ☐ —#1 MJ Wax Design Tool
- ☐ —one or more wax melting pots
- ☐ —MJ Circle Craft Templates
- ☐ —MJ Mini Square Craft Templates
- ☐ —MJ Mini Oval Craft Templates
- ☐ —MJ Mini Circle Craft Templates
- ☐ —Flex-e Ruler
- ☐ —MJ Dry Board
- ☐ —tray
- ☐ —drill or Dremel
- ☐ —³/₃₂" drill bit
- ☐ —jigsaw or gourd saw
- ☐ —Crayola crayons in colors White and Metallic Steel Blue
- ☐ —black acrylic paint
- ☐ —black spray paint

- ☐ —varnish
- ☐ —E6000
- ☐ —flat red stones
- ☐ —⁶/₃₂ paper rush
- ☐ —7-ply Irish waxed linen in turquoise and white
- ☐ —rubber finger protector
- ☐ —2 tapestry needles, size 18
- ☐ —paintbrush
- ☐ —scissors
- ☐ —hobby knife
- ☐ —white charcoal pencil
- ☐ —Mr. Clean Magic Eraser
- ☐ —cotton balls
- ☐ —Q-tips
- ☐ —paper towels
- ☐ —water container
- ☐ —toothpicks

Preparing the Gourd

For this project you can use any type of round gourd. Kettle gourds, also called martin gourds, would work as well.

Using an MJ Circle Craft Template, find the circle that fits well on the top of the gourd. Trace around the inside of the circle template with your white charcoal pencil. Use removable glue dots if you need help holding the template on the gourd.

Cut the top with your jigsaw or gourd saw. Sand the rim of the gourd nice and smooth so the waxed linen does get caught on the gourd. The rim should be flat. Lightly sand the side inside edge of the rim.

Using the ½" Flex-e, wrap it around your gourd and measure the holes. You want the holes ½" down and ¾" apart, and for this project you want an odd number of holes for the gourd design. Adjust the spacing if needed. (If you are only doing the Arrowhead Points rim and not the rest of the design, you don't have to worry about the number of holes in the rim.)

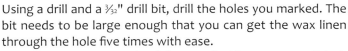

Using a drill and a ³⁄₃₂" drill bit, drill the holes you marked. The bit needs to be large enough that you can get the wax linen through the hole five times with ease.

Base-coat the outside of the gourd with two coats of black acrylic paint. Varnish the gourd with one coat of varnish to keep the gourd clean and protected.

If you want a design that is even, like the gourd design pictured here (not referring to the rim design), measure the rim around the gourd. Divide the gourd in half. Measure each half, placing the holes ¾" apart. You may have to adjust a little. By dividing the gourd in half first, your gourd will always have an even number of holes.

Arrowhead Points Coiled Rim

Measure the length of paper rush needed for the rim by loosely wrapping the paper rush around the rim of your gourd five times, which is the number of rounds for the rim, plus include some extra. It is always better to have too much instead of not enough.

1.

With your scissors, cut the first part of the paper rush on a long, very slanted (tapered) angle. It looks much better when adding the next row. It blends in more.

The Irish waxed linen that is used in the project is made up of 7 strands. The most common waxed linens are 4-ply. By using the 7-ply cord, the project is heavier and can be completed much faster. I strongly recommend using the 7-ply cord for this project to make the pattern work correctly. This waxed linen can be purchased from Royalwood, Ltd.; see the suppliers list at the back of the book.

Using the white waxed linen, cut off a piece of cord as long as you are comfortable working with. I use about a six-foot piece. Thread it through the tapestry needle.

A tapestry needle works best because it does not have a sharp point and will not get stuck in between the strands of waxed linen and make a mess. It also keeps you from poking your finger with a sharp point.

2.

Push the needle through one of the holes from the front of the gourd to the inside. Pull the cord through leaving a 5" tail. The tapered end of the paper rush should sit between this hole and the hole to the right. The slanted part of the paper rush should be facing up.

Tie a double knot nice and tight. The paper rush should be sitting on the cut edge of the rim. Slide the knot to the back of the paper rush so that it does not show. This will count as one long stitch in the hole.

If you are doing a different gourd design and already have your gourd finished, you would want the starting position of the rim in the back of the gourd design.

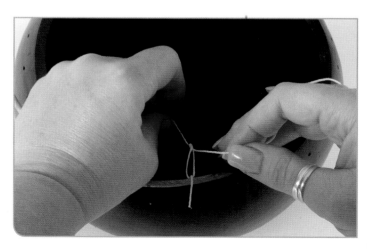

3.

Lay the tail of the cord on the edge of the gourd with the paper rush. It should be toward the inside so that it does not show. As the stitches are made over the paper rush, the tails will be covered as well. Take your needle and go under the paper rush to form a small loop (wrap) around it. Pull the loop nice and tight. You are working in a clockwise direction.

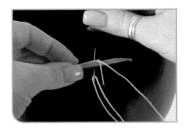

4.

Pull the cord from the top and with your needle go through the front of the same hole to form the second long loop.

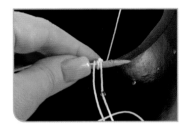

5.

Pull the needle out the back of the hole. Bring the needle up and wrap around the paper rush (second small loop). Pull the cord tightly.

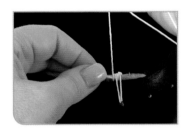

6.

Bring the needle down to the hole and push it toward the inside forming the third long loop. Your needle should always be coming over the rim from the inside and toward you.

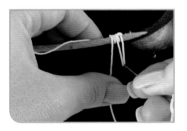

Pull the needle through the hole then up and wrap around the paper rush (third small loop). Pull the cord nice and tight.

7.

Bring the needle down to the hole and push it toward the back forming your fourth long loop. Pull the cord up from the back nice and tight.

Pull the needle out the back of the hole. Bring the needle up and wrap around the paper rush (fourth small loop). Pull the cord up from the back nice and tight.

8.

Now that the hole is starting to get tighter, you may want to put on your rubber finger protector. This helps you hold onto the needle while pulling it. It also gives your finger some protection.

9.

Bring the needle down to the hole and push it toward the back forming the fifth long loop. Pull the cord up from the back nice and tight. This is the last long loop in this hole. There will be a total of five long loops with a small loop in between each one. I will refer to this sequence as an arrowhead point.

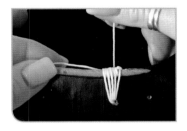

Adjust/move the paper rush slightly to the right so that the third long loop is in the center of the hole and straight up and down.

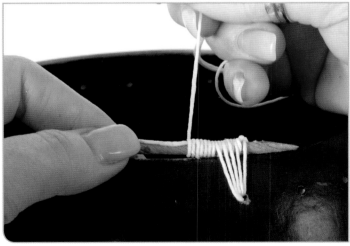

10.

Neatly wrap the cord around the paper rush several times between the holes. Check the inside of your rim to make sure that the loops are not overlapping and are laying straight. The inside of your rim should look as nice as the front of your rim especially if you are entering it into a competition.

You will have to adjust the number of small loops that you put between each arrowhead point. Generally, if you did ¾", you will have ten small loops. This will vary if you use a different ply of waxed linen or different size paper rush.

Keep the loops pushed nice and tight together. There should be no room in between them.

11.

To determine if you have enough small loops, pull the cord from the last small loop down to the next hole. The cord should lay down with not much space between the last short loop and the long loop.

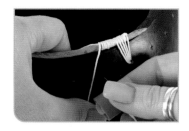

12.

Push the needle in from the front of the hole to form that long loop. Pull it up from the back nice and tight. The loop should be slanting from the right to the hole. Add a small loop next to the long loop. Remember to check the inside of the gourd to make sure the cords are laying straight.

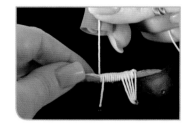

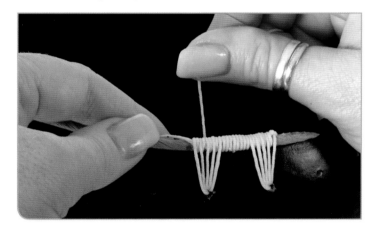

13.

Push the needle through the hole again to make the second long loop. Pull it up from the back tightly. Repeat small and long loops until you have a total of five long loops in the hole or an arrowhead point. This is very important for the design to look good. If the middle long loop is not straight up and down in the middle you need to adjust the small loops. If it is more toward the left, take out all the loops until you get to the ten smaller loops. Take out one or two small loops and then do the arrowhead point pattern again. If the middle long loop is leaning to the right you may need to take out the long loops and add more little loops and then add the arrowhead point again. I cannot tell you how import it is to learn how to adjust the design. Never be afraid to take a section out and adjust it. It will make all the difference in the end.

Remember that tail that you have been covering up with the loops? Go ahead and trim it off next to the last loop. You want to make sure that the tails are covered up by about two inches of stitches before you trim the tails to keep them nice and tight and in place.

14.

Continue the design around the rim, adjusting smaller loops when needed, but never alter the five long loops. They are the arrowhead point design.

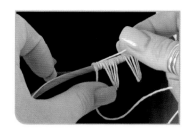

When there is only twelve inches of cord left, stop no matter where you are in the design. Cut another six-foot piece of the cord. Lay the new cord, with at least a 1" tail on the new cord, to the right on top of the previously worked stitches. Keep making your loops right over the top of the tail of the old cord keeping it toward the inside of the rim.

15.

Continue making several loops over the rim, until you have created at least 1" of loops over the new cord and still have a 3" to 4" tail on the old cord. Slowly!! Start to pull the new cord until all of the

tail is completely under the loops and stop pulling. If you pull too fast it may come all the way out. If this happens, undo the loops and do it again.

16.

Lay the end of the old cord onto the rim and pull the new cord up from the back and continue doing your loops where you left off. You will continue covering the tail of the old cord as you go, keeping it on the inside of the rim.

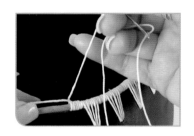

17.

Remember to keep checking the design on the inside of the rim. Do not be afraid to use your needle and straighten out any cords that overlap or are not close to each other.

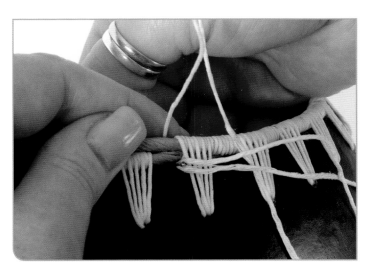

18.

Complete all of the rim design on the first row except the last hole. Continue with the design until you meet up with the tapered end of the paper rush.

The paper rush should be at a slant. Start to wrap over the end of it with the loop that you are currently working on. Pull the cord nice and tight. Make sure that you are putting the needle under both pieces of paper rush. Pull these loops nice and tight, even more so in this area to help make the transition look smoother.

19.

You will continue putting the needle under both pieces of paper rush until you get to where the wrapping began. There should be no space between the last loop and the very first loop. The paper rush should be one on top of another.

20.

You can use this simple design by itself for a gourd. I have also used this around a gourd piece, as a jewelry piece or ornament.

21.

Take your needle and put it under only the top paper rush to create a small loop. You are only doing small loops on this layer of the gourd. No arrowhead points. Pull the cord nice and tight.

Do small loops all of the way across the top of the arrowhead point below. Once your last loop is over the last loop on the left of the arrowhead point, do one more loop and take the cord to the inside of the gourd. Keep the loops nice and tight.

22.

Insert the needle below the first row, through from the inside next to the last long loop of the arrowhead point. Pull the needle through the front. Keep it tight.

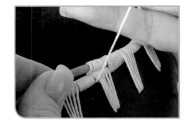

23.

Now insert the needle between the two pieces of paper rush (keep the stitch straight).

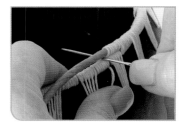

24.

Pull the cord up from the back. You want to keep these stitches as tight as possible so the cord that you put into the first row blends in instead of standing out.

25.

You have created a figure eight. This keeps the two rows sewn together. Make sure that your cord is going in the right direction when doing the figure eight. Refer back to previous steps if needed.

26.

Bring your needle over the top of the paper rush and insert needle between first and second row. Add small loops above the small loops below. Stop when you get to the right of the first long loop of the arrowhead point.

27.

Pull the cord up from the back and go under the paper rush toward the inside. Insert the needle below the first row and through from the inside, to the right of the arrowhead point. Pull the needle through the front. Keep it tight.

28.

Insert the needle between the two pieces of paper rush (first and second row), forming a figure eight. Pull the cord nice and tight.

Once you have completed the figure eight, start your

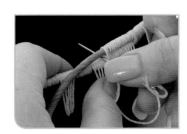

small loops across the top of the arrowhead point until you reach the other side of the arrowhead point. Continue around the rim placing a figure eight above the left side and right side of each arrowhead point.

29.

Once you have completed row two, start row three adding a figure eight directly above the figure eight in the row below.

30.

Add small loops in between the figure eights. Keep the figure eights directly above the ones you did on the last row. They should line up to the left and right of the arrowhead point on the first

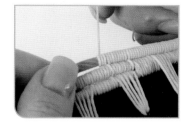

row. Complete all but the last area above the last arrowhead point.

31.

Cut a six-foot length of the turquoise waxed linen. Leave a 2" to 3" tail. Thread the turquoise waxed linen with your second needle. Continue adding your loops and figure eights going over the tur-

quoise waxed linen. Make sure you have covered the turquoise cord at least an inch or more.

32.

Slowly start to pull the cord. Remember to take this nice and slow. If you pull it fast and it comes out, undo the loops and start again. Pull until the tail of the turquoise cord is all covered up by the white cord. Stop pulling at this time.

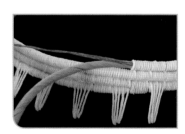

33.

Continue with the white small loops at the beginning of the fourth row. There are no figure eights in this row. Once you have gotten directly above the left side of the first arrowhead point you will start the turquoise arrowhead point. This will be directly above the figure eight you did in the last row. Lay the white cord along the top of the rim nice and tight and bring the turquoise cord over top the white cord. Start the arrowhead point with a little loop and a long loop. Do not cut the white cord. You will continue to use it.

At the end of the long loop, insert the needle in the middle of the area between the two arrowhead points on the first row. The needle will go between the first and second rows. You will see an open area that your needle will go into. Pull the cord from the back. Pull it nice and tight.

34.

Bring the cord over and push the needle under the paper rush to form a small loop. Pull the cord from the back nice and tight. Repeat until you have a total of five long loops with small loops in between each of those and one starting and ending the arrowhead point-for a total of six small loops. The last small loop is not yet been added in this picture.

The arrowhead points replace the figure eights in this row and are what keeps this row anchored. Make sure to keep the loops nice and tight.

35.

Lay the turquoise cord down along the rim, nice and tight. Pick up the white cord and bring it forward over the paper rush to form a small loop. You should have about the same amount of small loops as you did on the first row. You may have to adjust them just a little to keep the turquoise arrowhead points in the middle of the space between the bottom arrowhead points.

36.

Once you have added all the small white loops, start the next arrowhead point. Remember you should have a small turquoise loop at the beginning and end of each arrowhead point. This really helps maintain the symmetry of the design.

37.

After you have completed the arrowhead point, lay the turquoise cord down on the rim and pick up the white cord and bring it over the paper rush to form a small loop. Continue the design around the rim.

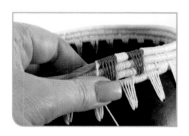

This is an example of the rim done with only four rows and the last row on top was only done with one color instead of using two colors. It is a little easier to create for that reason and you may like the solid color design on the rim better.

38.

Since the long loops take more cord, you will run out of the turquoise cord faster. Add it just like you have been doing. This is going to give you three cords you are carrying (maybe four if you are running out of white too). Lay the turquoise cord down on the rim leaving a 2" to 3" tail. Continue working on your design covering up the cord as you go. Try to keep the new cord toward the back of the design. When you have the cord covered up about an inch or more pull the cord until the tail is pulled under the loops on the rim. You can pick up the new cord when you get to the part of the design that is using turquoise. Loop the new turquoise over from the back and lay the old turquoise cord down on the rim next to the white cord.

39.

The inside of the rim design should look as good as the outside rim design. It is easier to keep it straight as you go. You can use your needle to straighten out the cord if needed.

40.

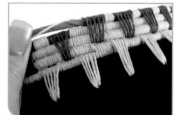

Complete the arrowhead points until you have completed the row. Your last arrowhead point should be directly above where you started the rim.

41.

Once you have completed the last arrowhead point, cut the remaining turquoise cord off with a 3" tail, laying it down on the rim. Pull the white cord over the top of the turquoise cord and the paper rush to form a small loop. Continue to add the small loops until you get to the right of the arrowhead rim.

42.

Do a figure eight with the white cord. Refer back if you need to for the figure eight. Make sure to pull the cord nice and tight. Add small loops until you reach the other side of the arrowhead point and do another figure eight. Continue adding small loops with figure eights on each side of the arrowhead points in the white cord until you have completed all but one inch of the rim.

43.

With your scissors cut the last inch of the paper rush at a gradual angle, so the cut side will be on the bottom. The beginning of the cut should be right at the beginning of the next row. The paper rush should be at such an angle that the paper rush, when covered, will blend into the last row and you should not see too much of a bump. Do not cut the paper rush too short. It is very hard to try and add some paper rush back on.

44.

Continue to add the small white loops until you get across the top of the last arrowhead point.

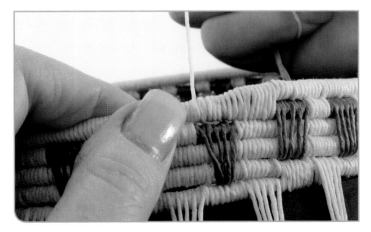

45.

Do a figure eight at the end of the arrowhead point. Pull it nice and tight. After the figure eight, loop your cord over the paper rush and the row below it. Pull the cord as tight as you can get it. Continue working down until you cover all of the paper rush. You should be directly above the end of first arrowhead point. Put in a couple of loops if needed to get to the side of the arrowhead point.

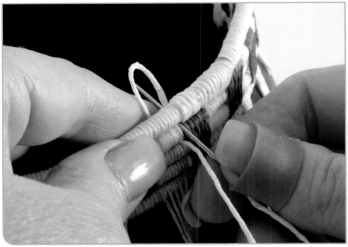

46.

Add a figure eight. Pull it nice and tight. With your needle, work under some of the loops to anchor the white cord. Pull the cord through and cut off any remaining tail.

47.

See the end of the rim? The top part could be a little smoother. There is a little bump on the last row. A longer, more gradual taper would make for a smoother ending. The front of the rim is where you want your design or any main focus. The rim should look as good on the inside as the outside of the design.

"Blue Horizons" Wax Design

To start the design on your gourd, get out your MJ Mini Square Craft Templates. Counting out from the middle of the square craft templates, pull out the third template. I do not use the diamond-shaped craft templates. Those come to too much of a point for this design. However, in these directions I'll be referring to "diamond shapes" or "diamond points" since that's what the shape is.

1.

You want to have the template reach from arrowhead point to arrowhead point. Have the square corners meet up with the arrowhead points. You can squeeze the template in with your fingers if it is a little too large. Trace around the inside of the template with your white charcoal pencil.

2.

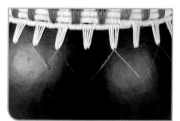

Start the design at the back and continue the design making the same number of diamonds in each direction.

3.

If you did an odd number of points or holes on the rim, when you reach the center front there are two arrowhead points remaining and two arrowhead points on each side. Counting from the middle of the MJ Mini Circle Craft Templates, pick out the fifth circle from the middle. Lay the template in the open area, reaching from the last point on the right to the last point on the left. You should use about half of the template. Using the white charcoal pencil, draw on the inside of the template. The half circle should meet up with the design on both sides. No open area should be between them.

4.

Switch to the MJ Circle Craft Templates, which are a larger set of circles. Pull the second one out from the middle. Lay it down about ½" from the last circle design. Try to keep it as evenly spaced from the first half-circle as possible. You will see that the ends do not meet up at the points. They start on the side of the diamond shape. Trace the inside of this circle with your white charcoal pencil.

5.

Pull out the fourth template from the middle of the circle templates. Lay it on the tips of the diamonds on each side, keeping with the shape of the inside circles. Trace the inside of the circle.

6.

Switch to the MJ Mini Oval Craft Templates. I know you have used a lot of different templates. Once you start using them you will wonder how you ever lived without them.

Pull the fourth template out from the middle. Start with the diamond shapes right next to the middle circles. Adjust the oval template so that the top of the oval is the same height as the last circle you did. Mark the template with your white charcoal pencil on each side where it meets up with the diamond points. Continue around the design. Starting where you marked the oval and placing it from point to point.

7.

Go all the way around the rim until you meet up with the half circle on the other side.

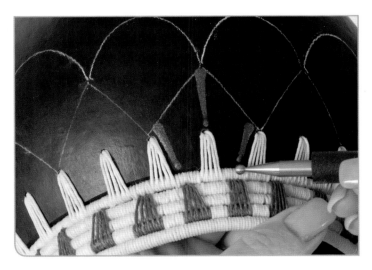

8.

I used a white crayon on this gourd with a steel blue Metallic FX Crayon. It is found in the Metallic FX box. I used a color that matched the color of the turquoise wax linen. I wanted to give the gourd some shine and sparkle but you give up the brightness of the color.

 Plug in two melting pots, having two will save you time and crayon. Start to melt the steel blue. You have to stir the wax a little more if has been sitting because the sediment added to this color will go to the bottom of the well. I used the MJ Wax Tool #2 but would most likely use the #1 tool large end next time for this area. Turn the gourd upside down so you are pulling the stroke toward you. Start at the point of the diamond and pull the stroke up to the arrowhead point. Try not to get wax on the arrowhead point.

 Pull a stroke to the right, next to the arrowhead point. Follow the shape of the arrowhead point. Stop when you reach the rim. Repeat on the left side. Make sure you reload your wax tool with each and every stroke.

9.

Go back in between the top stroke and the stroke on the right and place a stroke evenly in the middle of those. Repeat on the left side.

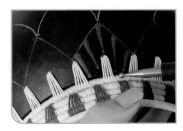

10.

On the right side, pull a stroke in between the top stroke and the middle stroke. Put a stroke between the middle stroke and the bottom stroke. This is the open areas you have left. Repeat on the left side.

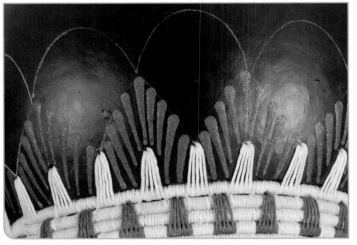

11.

Repeat on the next diamond shape. Continue until you have done all the diamond shapes around the top.

12.

Stop now, and remove only the diamond shape lines with your damp Mr. Clean Magic Eraser. It is easier to do it now than after the next layer of wax has been applied, making it harder to get in between the strokes to clean off the white charcoal pencil.

 Take a damp paper towel and remove the chalky film left by the Magic Eraser. Do not wipe the lines off the ovals.

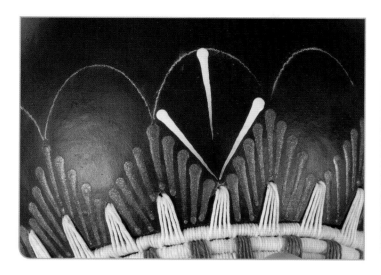

13.

Switch over to white crayon. Remember that white can drip a little more. It is better to put the white into the melting pot right before you use it, instead of letting it sit there and get warmer. If your white starts to drip after sitting too long, take some of the wax out of the well with a cotton ball, just a little. If it continues to drip, stir the white to cool it down with your wax tool.

Using an MJ Wax Tool #2 small end for a nice large stroke, turn your gourd upside down and pull the stroke down the center of the oval. Pull the stroke until it runs out of wax or you reach the bottom of the design where the two diamonds meet.

Starting on the right side were the oval meets up with the diamond point, pull a stroke until you run out of wax or you reach the bottom of the design where the two diamonds meet. Repeat on the left side.

14.

Go back in between the top stroke and the stroke on the right and place a stroke evenly in the middle of those. Repeat on the left side. Be sure to pull the strokes so they will meet up in the same place so the strokes form a point.

15.

On the right side, pull a stroke in between the top stroke and the middle stroke. Pull a stroke between the middle stroke and the bottom stroke. This is the open areas you have left. Repeat on the left side.

16.

Continue until you have completed all the oval shapes around the gourd.

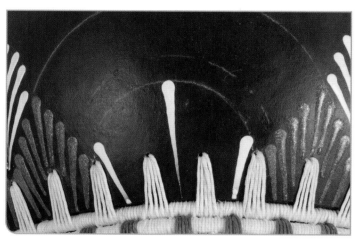

17.

Flip the gourd over and pull the stroke down the middle of the first inside circle toward you until you reach the rim or run out of wax. The tail of the stroke should go between the two arrowhead points. You should decide what size wax tool you want for this area.

Pulling the strokes toward you, pull a stroke on the right side just above the arrowhead point to the rim. Follow the direction of the arrowhead point. Repeat on the left side.

18.

Pull a stroke on the right in between the middle stroke and the bottom stroke. Pull the tail toward the arrowhead point. Stop when you reach it. Repeat on the left side.

19.

You should have enough room in between each of the strokes you did for another stroke. Complete the circle. Pull the wax until it runs out if you have room like the strokes in the middle. You can remove the white line you just used if you like at this time.

20.

Switch back to the steel blue wax. Pull a stroke starting at the next circle. Pull from the top of the circle line down in between each of the white strokes. You will have room. Most of the wax will be gone

before you get in between the white stokes. Pull as far as you can.

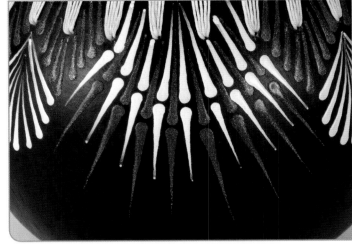

22.

Switch back to the steel blue. Pull strokes just a little down from the last set of steel blue strokes. Pull the strokes until you run out of wax. If you are loading your strokes the same each time, the strokes should all stop at about the same length.

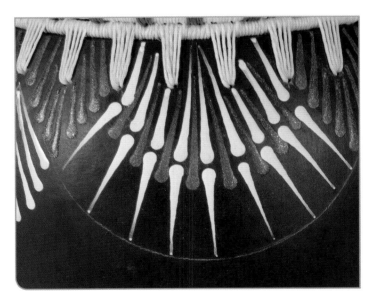

21.

Switch back to the white. Keep the gourd facing toward you; do not turn it upside down. Start just above the white strokes in the first row; pull the stroke out keeping the stroke following the same line out until you reach the last circle line. Do not touch the other set of white stroke; keep a little space in between the strokes. Try to keep these strokes as evenly spaced as possible. It is easier to start with the stroke in the middle and pull that one straight down. Start to work out from the sides starting in the middle.

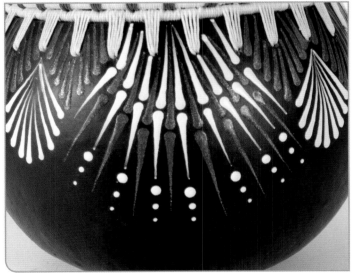

23.

Go back to the white wax. Add three descending dots. Start right after the end of the white strokes and dot, dot, dot, each dot will be smaller as the tool runs out of wax. Reload and do the next set of dots. This fills in the open area between the steel blue strokes. The dots complete the design.

24.

Back to the steel blue wax: Add three descending dots in between where the ovals meet together. Start these dots just above the strokes on the bottom. This will complete your design. Remove any white lines with the Magic Eraser. Touch up any areas needed with your basecoat color. This touch-up paint will stand out until you varnish it again.

25.

Use a brush-on varnish to varnish this gourd including a smaller brush to get up in between the arrowhead points. Do several coats. Let the gourd dry between coats of varnish. Use the dry board to place the gourd on to dry without sticking to the bottom of the gourd.

Next, you'll glue on flat bottom stones. They will help improve the design as well as cover up the tails to clean up the look. Use E6000 to glue on the stones. Keep the area you're working level so the stones don't slide. It takes a while for the glue to dry. You can glue a few stones on at a time, or you can glue and tape them on with painter's tape. Make sure the stones do not slip on you! Keep an eye on them for at least an hour.

26.

Glue three big stones in between the bottom of the front design to clean up the tails. It is amazing what a stone can do for a design. Select a color that will accent the design.

27.

Apply flat-bottomed small round red stones to the end of the tails on the white strokes. We keep a supply of flat stones at www.miriamjoy.com so that you can always find them.

Decide whether you like the even or the odd number design better. What colors would suit you better? What stones might you add to totally change the look of the design? What other design shapes would you like to try with the arrowhead rim?

Now you've learned a good variety of designs and how to apply them, along with very different rim treatments from simple to more complex, each adding so much to the design. Take this and build on it, adding your own personal touch or style.

Gallery

Wax design and photography by Miriam Joy except where otherwise noted

THIS PAGE: Wax design by Liz Drake, photography by Hal Eskew

91

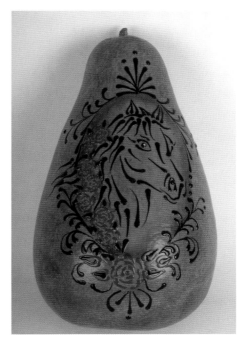

Suppliers

Raw Gourd Suppliers

Ghost Creek Gourds
Dickie & Linda Martin
www.ghostcreekgourds.com
864-682-5251

Pumpkin Hollow
Darrell and Ellen Dalton
www.pumpkinhollow.com
870-598-3568

Smucker's Gourd Farm
317 Springville Rd.
Kinzer, PA 17535
717-354-6118

Tom Keller Gourds
Tom & Zelda Keller
www.tomkellergourds.com
662-494-3334

Wuertz Gourd Farm
Waylon & Leah Wuertz
www.wuertzfarm.com
520-723-4432

Gourd Tools and Materials

Arizona Gourds
Bonnie Gibson
www.arizonagourds.com
520-477-7230

Artgal's Studio
Pine needles (natural and dyed), waxed threads, imitation sinew
www.artgalstudio.etsy.com
www.facebook.com/ArtgalStudio

Blue Whale Arts
Leah & Berry Reed
www.bluewhalearts.com
603-734-5504

The Canning Shop
Jim Widess
www.caning.com
800-544-3373

The Country Seat, Inc.
1013 Old Philly Pk.
Kempton, PA 19529
610-756-6124
www.countryseat.com

Giraffes Laff Art & Crafts
Bob & Sherry Briscoe
giraffeslaff@bellsouth.net
336-634-3397

Marianne Barnes
Author of books on weaving and gourds
www.maribasket.net
maribasket1@charter.net

Royalwood, Ltd.
517 Woodville Rd.
Mansfield, OH 44907
419-526-1630
800-526-1630
www.royalwoodltd.com

Should you need to contact me, please email me at
Art@miriamjoy.com. I make every effort to return your email within twenty-four hours of receiving it.

I can be reached through the social media websites listed below:

Facebook: **Miriam Joy's Waxy Crafty Corner**
Facebook: **Miriam Joy Gourd Creations**
Pinterest: **www.pinterest.com/miriamjoysagen**
YouTube: **www.youtube.com/user/Miriamjoy123**
Etsy: **https://www.etsy.com/shop/Miriamjoyscraftstore**

Thank you for purchasing this book and supporting my artistic ideas and products.

God bless,
Miriam Joy

Miriam Joy's Products and Supplies

I invite you take time visit the MJ products that I have featured in this book. I am constantly updating this page with new and innovative products for you to enjoy. The website with featured products can be found at **www.miriamjoy.com.**

I am constantly working on new projects and new YouTube videos for you. You can subscribe to my YouTube channel so that you can get all the latest videos on YouTube at Miriamjoy123 or type in the direct link **https://www.youtube.com/user/ Miriamjoy123.**

I also have a Facebook page at "Miriam Joy's Waxy Crafty Corner." I post pictures of projects and other craft items on this page for you to make and be inspired.

For your convenience I offer Paypal or any major credit card should you wish to purchase products from my website.